R.I.P.

THE FEDERAL RESERVE BANK

1913-2028

R.I.P.

THE FEDERAL RESERVE BANK

1913-2028

And Other Predictions

PETER WARD HERALD

To order additional copies of this book, contact:
Xlibris Corporation
1-888-795-4274
www.Xlibris.com
Orders@Xlibris.com
77985

CONTENTS

ACKNOWLEDGMENTS

Dedicated to my parents who taught me how to read, and to my teachers and colleagues who made it all worthwhile.

INTRODUCTION

A privately owned bank has control over you and everything that you own. If you want to know what's ahead, continue to read.

Tunnel vision seems to be the order of the day. My aim is to expand the outlook for 100 years. But my main thrust is the next 20 years. I have intentionally tried to minimize the astrological language because I hope everyone reads this book. This book is for those who want to know, not only for astrologers.

As you read you will realize that a massive wool has been pulled over you and it is difficult to break out of it. Decades of conditioning are hard to over come. You will see that government is a giant harvesting machine that operates almost automatically to separate you from your money.

Cycles are historical inevitability when applied to nations. The individual person is fleet footed and can avoid danger. Nations not so. Nations are carried forward by their own weight, hard to make sharp turns. Previous structural investments have a strong magnetism; it's hard to let go. It's hard for a government to let go of its sacred cows or sacred ideologies. The metaphor is a cornered animal, coiled to spring at its enemy. The focus is fixed and concentrated. Compare to, say, digging in ones heels to resist losing the ground already claimed.

If you like adventure and action, stay here. If you like peace and quiet, leave. If you want to protect your family, children, find a small town and resettle. Find a farming community with like-minded neighbors who desire peace, productive work and self-reliance in a cooperative framework.

The Federal Reserve now owns over $1 trillion of mortgage-backed securities, which is 45.6% of all assets owned by it. In 2007, mortgage-backed securities were only 0.6% of the Federal Reserve's total assets. Purchases are financed through the **creation** of additional bank reserves.

The Federal Reserve is very highly leveraged, much more than most banks. It is carrying $2,157 billion of debt on $52.8 billion of capital, giving it a leverage of 40.8-times more debt than capital. The mortgage-backed securities it owns are 19-times greater than the Federal Reserve's capital, meaning that if the true value of these assets is 5.3% less than their book value, the Federal Reserve's capital is depleted, effectively making it another insolvent institution. Therefore, the flow of market activity must stall to protect the Fed from writing down this paper.

Given that Fannie Mae is itself insolvent and most other mortgage generating federal agencies are not far from that same dire financial condition, it is reasonable to assume that the true value of these mortgage-backed securities is less than 94.7% of their book value. Consequently, the Federal Reserve is—on a strict accounting basis—broke. It remains liquid because banks continue to provide it with funding and because people continue to accept in commerce and use customarily the Federal Reserve's liabilities, i.e., the paper currency it issues. But jobs will not return nor will business flourish.

And one question. Is there a backup system for the Federal Reserve Bank? In a civilization that prides itself on preparation and backup, this is never discussed as far as I know. Days are numbered for the Fed. It's time to begin asking tough questions because it's later than you think. Perhaps, the backup system is a global institution like the World Bank or IMF. In other words, Monopoly money.

A school of hard money economists is champing at the bit to remake the economy so that it works and works right. The internet is the new Fountain of Youth; from it springs honest questions and honest answers. And the primary thought out there is "when will the Fed submit to a thorough audit"?

We arrived at this point due to an era of profound irresponsibility.
—B. Obama January 2009

The truth of the matter is that you always know the right thing to do. The hard part is doing it.

—Norman Schwarzkopf

"The popular notion that an increase in the stock of money is socially and economically beneficial and desirable is one of the great fallacies of our time."

—Hans F. Sennholz

"I believe that banking institutions are more dangerous to our liberties than standing armies . . . If the American people ever allow private banks to control the issue of their currency, first by inflation, then by deflation, the banks and corporations that will grow . . . will deprive the people of all property until their children wake-up homeless on the continent their fathers conquered . . . The issuing power should be taken from the banks and restored to the people, to whom it properly belongs."

—Thomas Jefferson

I have covered a lot of ground in this book; I try to keep it trim and efficient. Because your time is precious and a word to the wise is sufficient.

P. W. H.

CHAPTER ONE

AMERICAN DETOUR

Forty or fifty years from now the Federal Reserve Bank may reappear in Disneyworld as a funny or scary ride. It may even capture a special place at Ripley's Believe It or Not.

We can now put a date on the final breath of the Federal Reserve Bank system (FRB). By 2028 the negative (retrograde) Jupiter cycle that began in 1906 will finish and at least one of its creatures, the Federal Reserve Bank (FRB), will be vastly diminished or completely removed from the national picture. Jupiter rules business, banking, higher education and international arrangements. The important point to remember is that the negative Jupiter cycle influenced a myriad web of corrupt laws, finances, agencies and culture in the 20th Century. Ethics was of the worst kind and deception prevailed.

The human condition being what it is, the cycles of planets push us around like chess pieces for good or for ill. I hope this book will enlighten and not frighten. When the cycle turns positive after 2028, a new set of philosophies for living will arise in the mind of mankind.

The FRB is one cog in the wheel of a worldwide network of central banks. This network operates day and night to achieve one purpose: the colonization of the United States.

Author, Matt Taibbi, among others, does a fine job of detailing the frauds and scams endorsed by the FRB to forestall its demise.

To resist is futile; the cycle will run down in a timely manner taking the FRB with it.

According to Congressman Ron Paul, whose basic premise in his fight against the Federal Reserve Bank is Einstein's "Don't expect the people who caused a problem to solve it," 75% of people want to see the Fed audited. "The Fed will self destruct when it destroys the dollar", Paul said.

For comparison lets look at the natal charts of PR China and Russia CIS.

I use the October 1, 1949 national day of PR China. Jupiter in the birth chart is almost motionless as it has just turned direct in motion in the celestial zodiac from the point of view of the Earth. This says that the free market economy does not come about easily in China. The early years were marked with central government planning and dictatorial policy. To overcome food shortages the government forbade more than one child per family. The weaknesses of big central government planning soon became apparent. Gradually it dawned on the government itself that this was unworkable and unsustainable. The people wanted a chance to have a better life. As the years passed, progressed Jupiter gained speed in the positive cycle. China opened up and investments flowed in and exports poured out. I predict that China will gather more and more speed toward achieving an ethical, free market economy as the years go by. Yes, there will be bumps in the road and the growth rate must be rational. But the overall trend is universal opportunity to achieve a better standard of living. Already, starting and running a business in China is less difficult than in the US.

Russia CIS natal chart is almost the opposite. The natal Jupiter is positive but slowing down to stationary retrograde cycle (negative) in just a few short years. I use the chart of national day December 25, 1991. A free market economy is the goal. Russia's free market system will always be overshadowed by the central government. There will be a lot of waste, interference and red tape in every direction of national life. The government does not play fair with foreign investors (oil drilling, for example). It's not what you know, but whom you know. Another stab at government reform and a new Constitution is probably in the cards in the future.

Writing a book such as this, it's important to take a synthesis of all the prevailing factors and prior conditions into account. Leading into the 21st Century financial crisis the US generally had no domestic savings upon which to fall back on for help. The US is dependent on foreign governments for rescue. There can be nothing more precarious than this. Indeed, the average American was deeply in debt and savings were "negative". Business depends on a regular flow of credit. The fractional banking system constantly adds more money into the monetary base thus devaluing the dollar. This is why, when all the factors are added up, the financial crisis with us since 2000 is permanent. (One might put it back to the Long Term Capital Management failure in 1998.) The American monetary philosophy of debt (negative cycle) is causing the US to become damaged goods. The interest on debt reaches a point that it becomes non-payable. This means that slowly but surely, most employment as it is understood today will eventually cease to exist. The Dollar slowly reduces to zero.

The government could, I suppose, seize by law all the remaining assets of Americans to keep the ponzi scheme going for a few more years. A negative Jupiter cycle dies a horrible death. Bailouts, stimulus and aid packages simply don't work because the people no longer believe in it. They can *sense* that it is over (positive Jupiter cycle vibrations in the early stages). But when those assets are used up, what next?

In a Bloomberg interview, Marc Faber—publisher of the *Gloom, Boom & Doom Report*—said within five years, 50% of taxpayer funds will be used just to cover the interest payments on the government's debts (a function of a ballooning balance sheet and higher interest rates). At that point, the government's only choice will be to monetize that debt, and that, Faber said, "will be the end essentially."

Faber's argument for inflation is simple: As long as the Federal Reserve has a money printer, all prices will eventually go up. For every new dollar printed into existence, the value of each existing dollar falls. Therefore, you need more dollars to buy the same asset. But prices increase faster than inflation when you're dealing with assets whose supplies can't increase at the same rate as paper money—assets like wheat, gold, oil, and so forth.

Or the Federal government could start the (inevitable) unwinding process immediately and relinquish controls on the free market. After 2028 a small business, small banking and free enterprise economy is more likely to prevail, anyway. By my calculations it is wise to cut government spending now, gradually but resolutely. As the government reduces taxes and downsizes itself, a revitalized free market can absorb the unemployed. That's the whole point of this political exercise anyway, isn't it? Getting people back to work? Or am I missing something?

The ramifications of delaying this decision to downsize are enormous.

Like a snake eating its own tail, the federal government is very close to being an employment-security agency. It's like a riddle wrapped in an enigma, a hybrid of Byzantine bureaucracy plus financial service center in Washington. It is a corporation government with lots of mass media propaganda. Unopposed, the government will control most large businesses not just the auto industry, insurance and banks. This costs money. This is what the end game of the negative business cycle looks like, a doomed creature that would feast on healthy tissue to stay alive.

But the cost is huge and the inflation that follows will dwarf anything that has ever been seen before. Hyperinflation is the final solution to expedient financial solutions such as this.

Based on the cycle of the *minor progressed* Venus (in the US birth chart), the next big inflationary danger to the economy is 2023 or a year or two earlier. The minor Venus by progression turns to the negative (retrograde) cycle every 21 years approximately. A quick review of the past years shows Venus minor negative in 1980 and again in 2001. I anticipate in 2023 a destructive inflationary period about 100 times greater than the late 70s, early 80s. Venus began negative cycle in 1958 but because the US budget and American households were in excellent fiscal shape, there was no great disruption. This is the lesson to be learned about the negative Venus cycle—sound finance and balanced budgets prevent economic dislocations and runaway inflation.

The US economy is unbalanced and so the pains of this *minor progressed* Venus cycle will be severe. Apply a remedy now and the pains will be less severe. It's as simple as that. We take our medicine now or take our chances later. The source of the pain is the budget deficit and paving over problems with printing press money.

Being aware of the positive and negative cycles provides planners, administrators and economists with the information that they have been missing and lamenting—WHEN.

The years between 2010 and 2016 are never worry free. Some states, like California, may go bankrupt (2012). This and other shocks will keep the markets jumpy. Government will subsidize and bailout the nation. The strategy is to wait out the storms by printing trillions of dollars of fiat currency. Everything is stagnant; there is no improvement in employment or business creation. The interest on the debt climbs.

The US begins a second major recession at the end of 2010 and into 2011. The stock markets will crash earlier in 2010, but recover in a strange manner. The government may over-regulate the stock markets causing panic and euphoria simultaneously. Nothing feels right. It is like watching a stage drama at a distance.

2017 seems to be a critical year. An ominous eclipse will cover the nation from West to East. The Vernal Equinox chart displays a rather ugly Moon Saturn conjunction in the 10th house of government. (It is reminiscent of the Vernal Equinox chart of 1945, the worst year of WW2 as far as US casualties are concerned.) Finally, a very important cycle comes to a close. Negative Mercury cycle will slow down during 2017 to reverse direction. Turning positive might seem to be a good thing except that as it slows down, massive decision making errors could occur in an already difficult year. Disturbing information also leaks out.

If attempts to balance the budget are unsuccessful foreign governments refuse the dollar. The dollar begins a descent to zero value and interest rates rise. By 2023, serious inflation compounds the problems. Since the government is the biggest employer, business and services shut down. Read the chapter regarding Solar Eclipses and the US territory.

At this point I will bring China into the picture. In 2017 China faces a financial crisis in the form of an inflationary depression. Major progressed Venus will conjunct major progressed Jupiter. The US credit crisis commenced under a similar planetary aspect in 2008. The economy appears to be a bubble and it will probably explode in June of 2017. I also note that *minor progressed* Venus will turn to retrograde negative cycle that same year in April. This is typically an inflationary indicator. Both of these events indicate a reversal of fortune for China. A serious stock market crash is likely. With so many ills facing America and China, the global picture looks very sour. The commodity and basic materials markets suffer downturns. What is the safe haven? It would have to be gold and silver, precious metals in general.

So that is 2017, just seven years from now as I write this. Leaders supporting the policy of smaller government and fewer "benefits and handouts" are the hope of a viable future. Also, a study should be made regarding all Executive branch appointments to critical offices. In other words, more scrutiny of the total government is necessary.

I have studied the underlying principles of national growth and change. The underlying factors extend for generations and centuries. One thing stands out sharply: the US is off course since 1906 and the challenge is to set the nation back on the right track by understanding that this aberration is coming to a close in 2028 and the politicians/international bankers have an Achilles heel. Namely, the tide is turning against them!

My research finds for those who condemn the recent series of administrations and policy makers in Washington, DC. It finds for those who launch scathing attacks against the Federal Reserve Bank and various other government agencies, such as Fannie Mae. My research also tends to confirm that those who are worried about the social trends in the nation are right to be worried, as the trends are indeed unwholesome and abnormal. Finally, my best estimate is that hardly anyone in Washington is telling the truth. Several factors are in play, including the already mentioned long term negative (retrograde) Jupiter cycle. I will discuss the negative Mercury cycle in another chapter of this book.

At the beginning of the 20th Century, due to a combination of ignorance, foolhardiness and greed a powerful, select group initiated actions that propelled the US into an empire like status for which it was not designed. This group, lacking intelligence for spiritual or ethical matters but consumed with worship of money has caused so much harm it will take a masterful effort of will to over come.

The United States was not designed to engage in a never-ending set of wars decade after decade. Nor is the monetary system designed to operate as a world reserve currency based on this empire concoction. This venture creates a kind of master-slave relationship between nations and peoples. The chain reactions of this foolish scheme are more and more apparent and dire now and as things develop in the future. The century long inflationary bubbles and deflationary pains are but one set of symptoms. The select group may be some sort of international conspiracy but that is not relevant. They are well entrenched now but certainly confused about what is happening to their schemes and the US. The scheme is going awry. The plot is failing because it was built on sand—the negative Jupiter cycle.

The first panacea for a mismanaged nation is inflation of the currency; the second is war. Both bring a temporary prosperity; both bring a permanent ruin. But both are the last refuge of political and economic opportunists.—Ernest Hemingway

With the use of pattern recognition techniques, I will explain why certain financial systems, international organizations and cultural trends must come to an end as dominant policies and ideas become obsolete over the next quarter century. The underlying factors indicate that this is terminal. I repeat, the financial and political world you see around you today will disappear within 25 years. No more too big to fail banks and insurance companies, quasi-government agencies and the price-of-money fixing Federal Reserve Bank system. The Federal Reserve Notes we use today will vanish.

Some of this may sound impossible. However, the overarching premise is: Most of the 20th Century banking/government/media axis was contrived to enrich a handful of people at the expense of national comfort and peace and quiet. And most of all, the loss of personal liberty and prosperity is the price for the continuity of this amazing deceit. As the pretenses attract spotlights due to Internet exposure and the gradual "sensation" of the positive Jupiter cycle coming into power, freedom of movement, speech, etc. suffer more and more restrictions to keep the game from falling apart. To maintain the general ponzi scheme, more and more debt and fiat printed money is needed. This is called looting.

This is the nexus of the problem: to preserve the old order, the nation will be wrecked unless the elite captains of "spindustry" are voted out of office. But more importantly, the dollar must be fortified with balanced budgets starting today.

Government bailouts of investment banks and other financial companies should be a clear warning alarm of icebergs ahead. Polls say most Americans disapprove of such taxpayer burdens. Governmental interference makes a mockery of free market capitalism. There is no free market now and hasn't been for many years. This interfering government is a creature born in a long-term negative cycle within the larger cycles that I research. In some ways the US is like a monarchy.

The underlying factors I speak of can also be understood as planetary influences. I will use these terms interchangeably. But it would be a mistake to equate my research with the popular notion of sunsign Astrology in vogue today. There is simply no comparison.

The 1906 planetary "influence" that ushered in the wrongheaded banking and perennial war system is now slowing down (as a potent influence) and going to reverse course in 20 years. The cycle is objective knowledge in mathematical terms. And it is palpable in a subconscious mental way that thinking people do tune into as they ponder larger issues. Once the general public becomes aware of the false and destructive nature of our "system" they are compelled to demand a change. More and more the "feeling" of the end of this cycle will prompt questions about what shall replace it. And that is the major national discourse that must take place soon.

In light of this imminent reversal of the trend, the resentment of politicians and banking cabal can already be felt strongly and this resentment can only increase as the days and years go by. They will push harder to make their ponzi dreams a permanent fixture in law and practice even after 2028. This willfulness will conflict with the forces of the positive Jupiter cycle that is bearing down upon them and the society as a whole. The conflict will probably assume physical manifestations as the years go by.

The usage of pattern recognition to decipher trends is objective knowledge. In fact, astrology is objective knowledge when looked upon as pattern recognition. Planetary movements are in repetitious mathematical cycles from the point of view of earth. This is the long range objective way to understand the ups and downs of civilizations, doctrines and cultural trends.

The USA has a birth chart. The Declaration of Independence is the birth of the USA. Astrology employing the astronomical positions of the planets describes the exact timing of the beginning and end of cycles or patterns. This is why I call it pattern recognition. Positive and negative cycles are recognized patterns using the astrology I have developed to understand our present circumstances and the length of time it takes to evolve from one set of circumstances to another set.

A business and cultural cycle massive in terms of time-length and influence in the affairs of the US went negative in 1906. But it was slowing down for two decades previously and so its effect was subtle at first and then increasingly disruptive. By looking back over 100 plus years in history we can clearly see how huge this cycle is and the ramifications it has had on our culture, opinions and financial well-being.

All cycles must come to an end. This negative cycle is now slowing down, and by 2028 will stop completely and reverse "course" to begin the positive side of the Jupiter cycle. The total length of this cycle, the negative part, is about 120 years, not including the several years before and after when the cycle slows down to change direction. Thus, these transition years are very critical and loaded with upheaval. If you think the present times are unsettling, just wait a few more years. Most if not all of the institutions built up during the 20th Century will come tumbling down.

It is the intent of this book to suggest a careful, rational deconstruction of those institutions so as not to unnecessarily disrupt life and living more than necessary. I am talking about very big institutions that affect every aspect of our lives. There is not enough money in the world to keep this deconstruction from happening. The continuing bailouts of the decaying banking, financial and industrial system will only destroy America in the long run. That it will happen, the deconstruction, is unavoidable; but if the advocates of the Austrian School of sound money economists step forward and advise, the transition will be less shocking. Naturally, the Keynesians must sit down and shut up.

I completely agree with the Austrian School. The classical liberal way of operating an economy makes profound sense and is the only way out of this cul-de-sac.

When the negative cycle began early in the 20th Century, the US was more agrarian, prosperous and certainly more self-sufficient than it is today. Diversity of enterprise was practiced, not just preached.

—

The nation as a whole kept a balanced budget and used sound asset-backed money on a daily basis. The US was also a peace-loving nation, not counting the Spanish American war and frontier battles. I believe the ludicrous war with Spain was the result of the negative Jupiter cycle taking hold. Many forget that the typical household needed only one breadwinner in the family. And multi-generational families looked after each other, young and old. This is a perfectly normal and ethical way of living.

Anyway, the US was very different. There was no inflation. That's right, there was no inflation. Prices were stable. The money supply was backed by gold. Most people worked for themselves. Immigration was carefully regulated. Politicians didn't make a career out of holding office; government was small and tidy.

The United States had a positive Jupiter cycle at the outset of nationhood until 1906.

Only the monetary policy of the 20th Century will be modified or discarded. The obligation of the US government to issue money, and not the FRB, will be restored. The basic foundation of the US is not affected. We are not a totalitarian dictatorship. Quite the contrary. Yes, the size of government will be affected, but not the original Constitution and Bill of Rights. The federal government will get much smaller in keeping with the original intent of the early Americans for minimal government and a free market economy.

Let me repeat, the US will remain a constitutional republic; it will not be an empire or major world player. It will be like it was in the 19th Century politically and economically with today's modern conveniences (depending on energy supply and invention). The citizens will conduct business with local small banks in modest cities and small towns; self-sufficient ways with electronic communications resume. It will have all the marvels of technology, modern energy production and wholesome agrarian, efficient urban living.

The subtle subconscious influences of this positive direct in motion Jupiter cycle will expose the errors of thinking of the past century. The US will not be involved in world affairs; it will be like a neutral state importing and exporting goods, not policing the world, just defending its borders. The government of the people, not the international banking conglomerates, will control the money supply.

A credible tangible asset will back the money. In other words, the US dollar will be worth something again, as it did in the 19th Century.

As you read my book I would like each reader to hold a thought in mind without having to accept it as truth. That thought is simply this: early on in the 20th century the US financial economy was hi-jacked by a cabal of foreign and domestic schemers. They tricked our government into creating the Federal Reserve Bank and later on other agencies. They gradually corrupted our government. They convinced the leadership to drop gold backed money for worthless paper and other debt instruments. They caused the Great Depression (credit manipulation) and pushed forward "remedial" socialistic schemes. They urged the nation to enter world wars. They bonded the banking system to the government. They foisted the theme of "too big to fail" on the public. They placed multi-generations of Americans in debt.

As I mentioned, we now have a time frame for this financial sickness of which the FRB is but a symptom. The dysfunctions of the US will dissipate within 20 years. However, it would be better to expose, study and discard the international mindset that afflicts the US before the natural timely conclusion of this negative cycle. Why? Because time is of the essence. Assortments of fiscal and social dangers are gathering in the gloom ahead. Why perpetuate huge budget deficits that will sabotage economic survival? Why maintain a dead or zombie fiscal machine for longer than necessary?

The end is written in the mathematics of planetary cycles, and the cycles cannot be repealed. But the cunning banker establishment here and abroad will do everything necessary to loot what is left of the US treasure. And the Trojan horse is called the Federal Reserve Bank.

For the US the age of globalism is all but over. I define globalism as that philosophy which destroys self respect and replaces it with the worship of central government. The negative philosophy or doctrine that supported such thinking is losing strength. The US should leave the UN and other international bodies, like the World Bank and IMF as well as terminate the Federal Reserve Bank system in well thought out stages.

In a moment of weakness the US entered a place of erroneous decision-making. Entered is not the best word; the US was misdirected into a place where errors could be made without detection. For the banker cabal, the errors resulted in greater profit. These errors produced an international or globalist mindset that has turned into a parasitic and toxic semi-police state shrouded in secrecy.

The Detour in the title refers to leaving the path of just and honest free enterprise civilization and entering the poorly lit and misleading signage road of global banking collectivist monopoly. The massive bank corporation has succeeded in fixing the price of money worldwide. It is also a part of a larger cultural design to reduce the human race to a form of servile feudalism without dignity.

Globalism is a fraud. It is essentially a malformed philosophy that attempts to control the universe. One can attempt to comprehend the larger picture but globalists have the audacity of seeking to control it. It is ugly, there is no other word for it. No wonder the world is full of wars, famines, fears and uprisings.

In the history of fiat or government-produced paper money, no fiat money in history has ever survived. The reason is that fiat money is produced (without the discipline of gold) in any quantities a government desires. When an economy slows or when a nation goes to war (which is always wildly expensive) the temptation to print the needed "funding" becomes overwhelming.

Eventually, the world distrusts fiat paper. In the end, each new issue of fiat money dies. The fate of the US dollar (Federal Reserve Note) will be no different. Gold backed money is the real reason why the 19th Century was a time of fiscal sobriety with balanced budgets.

It has not escaped me that this elite group of conspirators will not readily relinquish power. I know it sounds like a Nobody who watches planetary movements knows more about reality than the feet-on-the-ground, highly educated and super wealthy internationalists who pull the strings. And they have a large paid army of followers who will tear my arguments apart. As you wish. But don't say I didn't warn you about the upheavals to come. An ounce of prevention is worth a pound of cure. And let me repeat, people can feel the negative Jupiter cycle slow down, and it makes them think about things that are new and leads into novel questions.

The tempest in a teapot called "anthropogenic global warming" alarmists serves as a good microcosmic example of how those who would deceive for their own enrichment seek to pull the wool over the eyes. Just like the banker cabal tricked Congress into enacting the FRB in 1913, these "scientists" prepare fake statistics to support bad science. And before that they tried to foist atmospheric Ozone layer "holes" upon the mass media and scientific community. The banker cabal was just a lot more convincing.

"I contend that for a nation to try to tax itself into prosperity is like a man standing in a bucket and trying to lift himself up by the handle."—Winston Churchill.

CHAPTER TWO

CROSS OF GOLD SPEECH

William Jennings Bryan was a king-maker in the Democratic Party around the turn of the 20th Century. That means he could shift his support to a certain candidate who would surely get the nomination. He tried for the presidency but was considered too radical. Woodrow Wilson was one such beneficiary of Bryan's influence. One of Bryan's famous speeches given at the Democratic national convention of 1896 sums up the prevailing mood politically. As you read, you will notice there are some similarities with today's debates. You will also see that he recommended an income tax, a tax that all Americans should pay, not just the wealthy. Note that he was deeply affected by the approaching negative Jupiter cycle's big business and wheeler-dealer passions. On the one hand he loathes private central bank issued national money, on the other he argues for universal income tax to support big "protective" government. He was a corrupted Jeffersonian Democrat.

As I said before, the international banking elites capitalized on the confusion created by the on-rushing negative Jupiter cycle to fool Congress into passing the Federal Reserve Bank Act. The Panic of 1907 was also a vivid memory. In 1913 the government and the people were vulnerable to a sneak attack by the stealthy fiat money gang. It was not unlike the pleadings of Treasury Secretary Paulson for bailouts of the investment banks at the height of the Panic of

2008. Advocates for additional stimulus are still making noises today. The Fed has helped to destroy the American talent for discovery by logical analysis. The source of a problem is swept under carpets and throwing money at the problem is substituted. Indeed, logical analysis is the very antithesis of the Federal Reserve except as an argument for its own benefit.

The financial scheme that was presented in 1913 as the solution and prevention for all Future Panics has turned out to be of zero use in that respect.

Mark my words, the passing of the negative Jupiter cycle will create anew whirlwind passions as it dissolves over the next 20 years just as it spawned them over 100 years ago. Fear and disenchantment will shadow America with the breakdown of the fiat currency scheme. Gradual stark realism replaces the former dreamy hypnosis of effortless prosperity based on cheap credit and debt.

William Jennings Bryan, campaign speech, 1896

Mr. Chairman & Gentlemen of the convention: I would be presumptuous, indeed, to present myself against the distinguished gentlemen to whom you have listened if this was a mere measuring of abilities; but this is not a contest between persons. The humblest citizen in all the land, when clad in the armor of a righteous cause, is stronger than all the hosts of error. I come to speak to you in defense of a cause as holy as the cause of liberty, the cause of humanity.

When this debate is concluded a motion will be made to lay upon the table the resolution offered in commendation of the administration and also the resolution offered in condemnation of the administration. We object to bringing this question down to the level of persons. The individual is but an atom; he is born, he acts, he dies; but principles are eternal; and this has been a contest over a principle.

Never before in the history of this country has there been witnessed such a contest as that through which we have just passed. Never before in the history of American politics has a great issue been fought out, as this issue has been, by the voters of a great party. On the fourth of March, 1895, a few Democrats, most of them Members of Congress, issued an address to the Democrats of the nation, asserting that the money question was the paramount issue of the hour; declaring that a majority of the Democratic party had the right to control the action of the party on this paramount issue; and concluding with the request that the believers in the free coin age of silver in the Democratic party should organize, take charge of and control the policy of the Democratic party. Three months later, at Memphis, an organization was perfected, and the silver Democrats went forth openly and courageously proclaiming their belief, and declaring that, if successful, they would crystallize into a platform the declaration which they had made. Then began the conflict. With a zeal approaching the zeal which inspired the crusaders who followed Peter the Hermit, our silver Democrats went forth from victory unto victory until they are now assembled, not to discuss, not to debate, but to enter up the judgment already rendered by the plain people of this country. In this contest brother has been arrayed against brother, father against son. The warmest ties of love, acquaintance and association have been disregarded; old leaders have been cast aside when they have refused to give expression to the sentiments of those whom they would lead, and now leaders have sprung up to give direction to this cause of truth. Thus has the contest been waged, and we have assembled here under as binding and solemn instructions as were ever imposed upon representatives of the people.

We do not come as individuals. As individuals we might have been glad to compliment the gentleman from New York [Senator Hill], but we know that the people for whom we speak would never be willing to put him in a position where he could thwart the will of the Democratic party. I say it was not a question of persons; it was a question of principle, and it is not with gladness, my friends, that we find ourselves brought into conflict with those who are now arrayed on the other side.

The gentleman who preceded me [ex-Governor Russell] spoke of the State of Massachusetts; let me assure him that not one present in all this convention entertains the least hostility to the people of the State of Massachusetts, but we stand here representing people who are the equals before the law of the greatest citizens in the State of Massachusetts. When you [turning to the gold delegates] come before us and tell us that we are about to disturb your business interests, we reply that you have disturbed our business interests by course.

We say to you that you have made the definition of a business man too limited in its application. The man who is employed for wages is as much a business man as his employer; the attorney in a country town is as much a business man as the corporation counsel in a great metropolis; the merchant at the crossroads store is as much a business man as the merchant of New York; the farmer who goes forth in the morning and toils all day—who begins in the spring and toils all summer—and who by the application of brain and muscle to the natural resources of the country creates wealth, is as much a business man as the man who goes upon the board of trade and bets upon the price of grain; the miners who go down a thousand feet into the earth, or climb two thousand feet upon the cliffs, and bring forth from their hiding-places the precious metals to be poured in the channels of trade, are as much business men as the few financial magnates who, in a back room, corner the money of the world. We come to speak for this broader class of business men.

Ah, my friends, we say not one word against those who live upon the Atlantic coast, but the hardy pioneers who have braved all the dangers of the wilderness, who have made the desert to blossom as the rose—the pioneers away out there [pointing to the west], who rear their children near to Nature's heart, where they can mingle their voices with the voices of the birds—out there where they have erected schoolhouses for the education of their young, churches where they praise their Creator, and cemeteries where rest the ashes of their dead—these people, as we say, are as deserving of the consideration of our party as any people in this country. It is for these that we speak. We do not come as aggressors. Our war is not a war of conquest; we are fighting in the defense of our homes, our families, and posterity. We have petitioned, and out (sic) petitions have been scorned; we have entreated, and our entreaties have been disregarded; we have begged, and they have mocked when our calamity came. We beg no longer; we entreat no more; we petition no more. We defy them.

The gentleman from Wisconsin has said that he fears a Robespierre. My friends, in this land of the free you need not fear a tyrant that will spring up from among the people. What we need is an Andrew Jackson to stand, as Jackson stood, against the encroachments of organized wealth.

They tell us that this platform was made to catch votes. We reply to them that changing conditions make new issues; that the principles upon which democracy rests are as everlasting as the hills, but that they must be applied to new conditions as they arise. Conditions have arisen, and we are here to meet those conditions. They tell us that the income tax ought not to be brought in here; that it is a new idea. They criticize us for our criticism of the Supreme Court of the United States. My friends, we have not criticized; we have simply called attention to what you already know. If you want criticisms, read the dissenting opinions of the court. There you will find criticisms. They say that we passed an unconstitutional law; we deny it. The income-tax law was not unconstitutional when it went before the Supreme Court for the first time; it did not become unconstitutional until one of the judges changed his mind, and we cannot be expected to know when a judge will change his mind. The income tax is just. It simply intends to put the burdens of government justly upon the backs of the people. I am in favor of an income tax. When I find a man who is not willing to bear his share of the burdens of the government which protects him, I find a man who is unworthy to enjoy the blessings of a government like ours.

They say that we are opposing national bank currency; it is true. If you will read what Thomas Benton said, you will find he said that, in searching history, he could find but one parallel to Andrew Jackson; that was Cicero, who destroyed the conspiracy of Catiline and saved Rome. Benton said that Cicero only did for Rome what Jackson did for us when he destroyed the bank conspiracy and saved America. We say in our platform that we believe that the right to coin and issue money is a function of government. We believe it. We believe that it is a part of sovereignty, and can no more with safety be delegated to private individuals than we could afford to delegate private individuals the power to make penal statues or levy taxes. Mr. Jefferson, who was once regarded as good Democratic authority, seemed to have differed in opinion from the gentleman who has addressed us on the part of the minority. Those who are opposed to this proposition tell us that the issue of paper money is a function of the bank, and that the Government ought to go out of the banking business. I stand with Jefferson rather than with them, and tell them, as he did, that the issue of money is a function of government, and that banks ought to go out of the governing business.

They complain about the plank which declares against life tenure in office. They have tried to strain it to mean that which it does not mean. What we oppose by that plank is the life tenure which is being built up in Washington, and which excludes from participation in official benefits the humbler members of society.

Let me call your attention to two or three important things. The gentleman from New York says that he will propose an amendment to the platform providing that the proposed change in our monetary system shall not affect contracts already made. Let me remind you that there is no intention of affecting those contracts which according to present laws are made payable in gold, but if he means to say that we cannot change our monetary system without protecting those who have loaned money before the change was made, I desire to ask him where, in law or in morals, he can find justification for not protecting the debtors when the act of 1873 was passed, if he now insists that we must protect the creditors.

He says he will also propose an amendment which will provide for the suspension of free coinage if we fail to maintain the parity within a year. We reply that when we advocate a policy which we believe will be successful, we are not compelled to raise a doubt as to our own sincerity by suggesting what we shall do if we fail. I ask him, if he would apply his logic to us, why he doesn't apply himself. He says he wants this country to try to secure an international agreement. Why does he not tell us what he is going to do if he fails to secure an international agreement? There is more reason for him to do that than there is for us to provide against the failure to maintain the parity. Our opponents have tried for twenty years to secure an international agreement, and those are waiting for it most patiently who do not want it at all.

And now, my friends, let me come to the paramount issue. If they ask us why it is that we say more on the money question than we say upon the tariff question, I reply that, if protection has slain its thousands, the gold standard has slain its tens of thousands. If they ask us why we do not embody in our platform all the things that we believe in, we reply that when we have restored the money of the

Constitution all other necessary reforms will be possible; but that until this is done there is no other reform that can be accomplished.

Why is it that within three months such a change has come over the country? Three months ago, when it was confidently asserted that those who believe in the gold standard would frame our platform and nominate our candidates, even the advocates of the gold standard did not think that we could elect a president. And they had good reason for their doubt, because there is scarcely a State here today asking for the gold standard which is not in the absolute control of the Republican party. But note the change. Mr. McKinley was nominated as St. Louis upon a platform which declared for the maintenance of the gold standard until it can be changed into bimetallism by international agreement. Mr. McKinley was the most popular man among the Republicans, and three months ago everybody in the Republican party prophesied his election. How is it today? Why, the man who was once pleased to think that he looked like Napolean—that man shudders today when he remembers that he was nominated on the anniversary of the battle of Waterloo. Not only that, as he listens, he can hear with ever-increasing distinctness the sound of the waves as they beat upon the lonely shores of St. Helena.

Why this change? Ah, my friends, is not the reason for change evident to anyone who will look at the matter? No private character, however pure, no personal popularity, however great, can protect form the avenging wrath of an indignant people a man who will declare that he is in favor of fastening the gold standard upon this country or who is willing to surrender the right of self-government and place the legislative control of our affairs in the hands of foreign potentates and powers.

We go forth confident that we shall win. Why? Because upon the paramount issue of this campaign there is not a spot of ground upon which the enemy will dare to challenge battle. If they tell us that the gold standard is a good thing, we shall point to their platform and tell them that their platform pledges the party to get rid of the gold standard and substitute bimetallism. If the gold standard is a good thing, why try to get rid of it? I call your attention to the fact that some of the very people who are in this convention today and who tell us that we ought to declare in favor of international bimetallism—thereby declaring that the gold standard is wrong and that the principle of bimetallism is better—these very people four months ago were open and avowed advocates of the gold standard, and were then telling us that we could not legislate two metals together, even with the aid of all the world. If the gold standard is a good thing, we ought to declare it in favor of its retention and not in favor of abandoning it; and if the gold standard is a bad thing why should we wait until other nations are willing to help us to let go? Here is the line of battle, and we care not upon which issue they force the fight; we are prepared to meet them on either issue or on both. If they tell us that the gold standard is the standard of civilization, we reply to them that this, the most enlightened of all the nations of the earth, has never declared for a gold standard and that both the great parties this year are declaring against it. If the gold standard is the standard of civilization, why, my friends, should we not have it? If they come to meet us on that issue we can present the history of our nation. More than that; we can tell them that they will search the pages of history in vain to find a single instance where the holders of fixed investments have declared for a gold standard, but not where the masses have.

Mr. Carlisle said in 1878 that this was a struggle between "the idle holders of capital" and "the struggling masses, who produce the wealth and pay the taxes of the country," and my friends, the question we are to decide is: Upon which side will the Democratic party fight: upon the side of the "idle holders of idle capital" or upon the side of "the struggling masses?" That is the question which the party must answer first, and then it must be answered by each individual hereafter. The sympathies of the Democratic party, as shown by the platform, are on the side of the struggling masses who have ever been the foundation of the Democratic party. There are two ideas of government. There are those who believe that, if you will only legislate to make the well-to-do prosperous, their prosperity will leak through on those below. The Democratic idea, however, has been that if you legislate to make the masses prosperous, their prosperity will find its way up through every class which rests upon them.

You come to us and tell us that the great cities are in favor of the gold standard; we reply that the great cities rest upon our broad and fertile prairies. Burn down your cities and leave our farms and your cities will spring up again as if by magic; but destroy our farms and the grass will grow in the streets of every city in the country.

My friends, we declare that this nation is able to legislate for its own people on every question, without waiting for the aid or consent of any other nation on earth; and upon that issue we expect to carry every state of New York by saying that, when they are confronted with the proposition, they will declare that this nation is not able to attend to its own business. It is the issue of 1776 over again. Our ancestors, when but three millions in number, had the courage to declare their political independence of every other nation; shall we, their descendants, when we have grown to seventy millions, declare that we are less independent than our forefathers? No, my friends, that will never be the verdict of our people. Therefore, we care not upon what lines the battle is fought. If they say bimetallism is good, but that we cannot have it until other nations help us, we reply that, instead of having a gold standard because England has, we will restore bimetallism, and then let England have bimetallism because the United States has it. If they dare to come out in the open field and defend the gold standard as a good thing, we will fight the to the uttermost. Having behind us the producing masses of this nation and the world, supported by the commercial interests, the laboring interests, and the toilers everywhere, we will answer their demand for a gold standard by saying to them: You shall not press down upon the brow of labor this crown of thorns; you shall not crucify mankind upon a cross of gold.

CHAPTER THREE

THE PSYCHIC FRONTIER

The Congressional Budget Office most conservative projections for continuing along the current (trillion dollar annual deficits) path lead to unsustainable deficit levels and bankruptcy for the country. According to CBO projections, debt will spike sharply upward in 2015, rising voraciously to over 700% of GDP in 2080. Of course, the economy will be destroyed and government forced to default long before then.

This governmental analysis seems fair and accurate in light of astrological timing. According to my interpretation of a number of indicators, by 2017 the US loses its coveted triple A credit rating and interest rates skyrocket. The nation has had this rating since 1917. Following that, the imports of needed goods falters and Americans must produce more domestically. By 2023 (minor) hyperinflation stalks the nation. And by 2088 a hyperinflation of 10,000 times greater than in 1980 destroys the nation completely.

The Western and Eastern economic systems depend upon an ever-increasing human population for its continued success. It is the largest "bubble" of all. At the final stages the required population growth is parabolic. A growing population of shoppers carries the human experience forward. Shopping, leisure activities, sports events and consuming food and drink maintain an internal combustion engine we call the economy. The educational system shapes children into wage earners and consumers. For those adults whose earning skills become crippled, the government provides subsistence living so they can at least spend.

The fiat money system creates a huge malinvestment in human reproduction. Therein lies the fatal flaw.

The latest federal and state dependence upon illegal immigration for the continuity of the American economy has reached its logical conclusion—the introduction of fresh consumer appetite to bolster the economy.

As if by clockwork, the United States stumbles into the same patterns that existed in the beginning of its birth to nationhood; an imperious government far away puts claims on the people under its control. The government I refer to is called the Federal government in Washington, DC. And it is far away because it is not in touch with rational economic principals. In the 1760s it was the British Empire—the Crown. And it was most definitely far, far away because it seems unable or unwilling to hear the reasonable voices of those people so locked into its machinations who dwell in the length and breadth of its colonies. The King and his Court were indifferent to the plea of the colonists for reduction of taxes. An exhausting war with France had bankrupted the Crown.

Within the United States itself, some people see through the façade of make believe liberty so carefully constructed and maintained. The clockwork is written in the sky, the return of transiting Saturn, Uranus (later on), Pluto and Jupiter to the places they occupied during the 1770s. Nostalgia for the long lost Republic awakens in the subconscious of the public.

The original structures of representational government, freedom and liberty created by the Founding Fathers remain intact and operational; however, the Executive Branch of government and all of the Cabinets and agencies it has spawned exists in a world of its own unfathomable intentions. The two party system built up over the decades does its bidding. And this insatiable breed careens in a headlong collision course with the rest of America just a sure as the colonists and the British Crown collided in 1775.

There are now so many problems in the USA that we don't know where to begin. So beyond the obvious ills afflicting our great nation we have a future of limitations awaiting us. And it is unavoidable; a domino effect, if I may call it that. A domino effect that is a chain reaction from erroneous, shortsighted decisions made decades ago and never corrected. Poor judgment and an escapist mentality pushed the troubles of yesteryear into the future. That future is now. A scheme (bailouts and quantitative easing and stimulus programs) to push the present ills forward into the future again is doomed to failure. There is no future dumping ground. A new timeline is imminent and it does not take IOUs.

Sometimes, I think that unborn intelligent life in the future is rejecting the policy of our present leadership to mortgage the future to pay the debts of the present. Does that make sense? It is like the unborn people don't want our crap anymore. The buck stops here; not in some future generation.

"This is where I have the greatest problem with US economic policy makers," writes financial analyst Marc Faber. "I don't think they have ever recognized that the excessive, credit-driven expansion of the US economy was unsustainable in the long run and that, sooner or later, the current crisis was inevitable."

There is only one way to kill capitalism . . . by taxes, taxes and more taxes.—Karl Marx

A new time means a new norm. However, if CAREFULLY SELECTED psychics advise the US leadership, some of these tragedies will be avoided or reduced, I think. I will discuss that happy possibility later. Within the term psychic I include astrologers, a separate kind of visionary who may or may not be psychic himself.

Scientists and other narrow-minded types will scoff at this suggestion. But scientists err when they attempt to overreach. They best remain in the material world where they belong. Many fine benefits to mankind are the result of science, of course. Their opinions about the finer intuitive faculties are irrelevant. Some of them don't even know if its hot or cold outside!

A government consulting gifted people is not out of the question. It can happen and I believe it must happen for the sake of a flawed monetary system and a tragically enfeebled people victimized by their leaders.

Elected officials and their appointees have betrayed Americans. A negative Jupiter cycle seems to block ethical responsibility. Democracy has failed because it only serves the politicians and their efforts to get re-elected. The latest efforts at this game of catering to special interest groups caused the biggest financial and economic disaster in recent history. I refer to governmental meddling in the housing and mortgage industry. The mega-colossal disruptions to follow in the years ahead will crush American civilization. The lust for votes causes it. The government only wants to save its own skin. (Don't believe me? Why have we not heard of the governmental "servants" of the people reducing their pay or salary and other benefits to help with the recovery? Does the expression "my fellow Americans" have a real meaning?)

The national debt evolves into a chaotic economy. The debt was caused by greed of perpetual office holders. Their "regulations" were self-serving regulations. The bribing of the electorate for votes creates massive national debts. Half the people are on "food stamps" (public assistance) because the government has taxed productive business out of existence. With no tax base the government goes abroad to seek loans from foreigners, thus our future is hocked to foreign governments. I don't know about you, but that to me is national suicide.

And Congress approved the Federal Reserve System so that we could have this?

Our gargantuan central government finally implodes and ruins millions of lives. There is no other way out. Eventually, the national territory is carved up and distributed to those who loaned the money. Americans are pushed out of their own homes to make room for foreign peoples who come to live here and create a new life for themselves in the "land of the free and home of the brave". Reservations are set up to care for the indigent and broke Americans. But they are not so cozy. Does this forecast ring any bells?

Politicians who are elected by lazy, dim-witted people looking for a handout cannot be taken seriously. They have no incentive to serve the nation as a whole; nor do they pass laws that safeguard the economic life and security of the nation. Re-election is all that matters to these parasites.

Pardon my harshness. I do hope we can work together in the future with cordiality and a common purpose—the preservation of the USA.

The Treasury Department force-feeds money into a moribund economy. The thinking is that since no one has savings nor good credit, its time to shovel money at the people and banks and hope some of it sticks to the marketplace so that goods and services start moving around again. It is also hoped that the prices of houses stop falling, falling and falling because nobody can sell houses any more or refinance mortgage loans. The amount of money, called stimulus, is going to become a second economy surrounding the original economy, like elaborate scaffold. Because of Federal government excesses, the superstructure that was once the free market is teetering; so a scaffold or "flying buttress" must support the thing. Meanwhile money is wasted doing this instead of simply providing loans for small business. We have the virtual world of the Internet; now we have the virtual economy. When you turn off the electricity, the Internet stops; when you turn off the loans from foreigners, the virtual economy stops.

Nixon ended the dollar link to gold convertibility in 1971. This was the heyday of the negative Jupiter cycle, the destruction of sound money at its peak. I didn't know it then but that was another nail in the coffin. Thereafter, the US Treasury could print as much paper money as it needed; paper money backed by nothing of value. The endless happy days are here again festival of Washington, DC was off and running. Do I believe the spiral of decay started in the 1970s? It depends upon what one is looking at. There is both good and bad practice in those years. The progressed planet Mars in the USA horoscope began to slow down in the 70s and 80s and came to a standstill in 2007. Aside from the negative Jupiter cycle, this is the factor that has really hurt the US over time. Our industry shrank and we didn't try to stop it. Did the nation get so blasé about the prosperity of future generations? Didn't anyone ask what would the next generations do for a living? Good manufacturing jobs lost; replaced with fast food and services not so well paying. We now have a government nationalizing bankrupt corporations to create a what me worry fantasy economy. The government now employs almost everyone in the public AND private sectors. It's not a free market, it's a ponzi scheme.

Public education is a farce. Can anyone read or communicate effectively? Is it time to revamp the teaching method?

It is almost impossible to save money; and it is not encouraged. The social security safety net is tenuous. To make ends meet, most people get trapped in the credit card syndrome.

I recall the phrases of politicians to do whatever it takes to get over this humongous economic crisis, even if it means breaking every rule in the book. I say, you should have had psychics in advisory positions so none of this bad planning would have gone this far. Foresight has been replaced with "just in time" simplistic, formulaic, mechanical, kick the bucket down the road thinking.

When foreign nations stop loaning money to America, the dollar will collapse and the nation will free-fall for a while. The dollar will collapse because the politicians will demand a paper money volcanic eruption that will result in serious inflation and social breakdown. They will demand printing press fiat money instead of facing the hard decisions. When things finally break down they can defend themselves by saying they had the best interests of the public in mind. Never mind that they know very well the consequences of evading problems by papering them over. And never mind that they caused the problems in the first place.

Generally psychics get a bad rap. Charlatanism is a word that comes to mind.

Scientists must be blamed for that, I suggest. Scientists are guilty of gross generalization about this and do not have the moral authority to venture an opinion there. Scientists thwart the proper educational curriculum that would produce a fine crop of psychics every year. Graduates who have a degree in psychic prediction improve society's chances for survival. Education must change in the future to allow for more talents in the mainstream of society. Imagine if AIG, Lehman Brothers, Citigroup, etc. had psychics on the Board of Directors. None of this mess would have occurred. Imagine a Psychic Security Agency existed. I guarantee 911 would never have happened; psychics would have sounded the alert years ahead of that tragic day.

Academia also must share the blame by kowtowing to scientists. Science and academia have grown so fat and smug that they have the peculiar ability to make people dull and stupid. And lastly, government lazily rubber-stamps their nonsense as acceptable for public consumption. The Establishment indirectly created these problems and the Establishment must be upgraded, improved and

R.I.P. The Federal Reserve Bank 1913-2028

refined. The psychic "nature" is a part of life; to deny it is tantamount to saying the Sun or gravity does not exist.

Contemplate this:

An example of the AMATEUR: "My education was of the most ordinary description, consisting of little more than the rudiments of reading, writing and arithmetic at a common day school. My hours out of school were passed at home and in the streets." Michael Faraday, who had little mathematics and no formal schooling beyond the primary grades, is celebrated as an experimenter who discovered the induction of electricity. He was one of the great founders of modern physics. It is generally acknowledged that Faraday's ignorance of mathematics contributed to his inspiration, that it compelled him to develop a simple, nonmathematical concept when he looked for an explanation of his electrical and magnetic phenomena. Faraday had two qualities that more than made up for his lack of education: fantastic intuition and independence and originality of mind.

"Professionalism is environmental. Amateurism is anti-environmental. Professionalism merges the individual into patterns of total environment. Amateurism seeks the development of the total awareness of the individual and the critical awareness of the groundrules of society. The amateur can afford to lose. The professional tends to classify and to specialize, to accept uncritically the groundrules of the environment. The groundrules provided by the mass response of his colleagues serve as a pervasive environment of which he is contentedly (sic) and unaware. The "expert" is the man who stays put". "The Medium is the Massage: An inventory of Effects" Marshall McLuhan. Bantam 1967.

Manufacturing must be revitalized and rebuilt from the ground up. Produce more high tech goods. Reduce the size of governments and repeal the taxation laws on business. Products start to leave the country at a lower price. Encourage a hospitable business environment. Eventually, the price finds acceptance abroad. We must think like an emerging market. Protect the workers; but tone down the frills. My suggestion as to the way out of this corner is simply that the US worker must become like a developing nation worker. We are essentially starting over.

—

Of course, there is the mad solution. The Mad Solution has the US declaring war on others in order to acquire raw materials and oil. This is done in order to avoid paying for anything. Thus the US becomes a gangster domestically and abroad.

Japan took that route in the 20th Century. Faced with currency and banking crises in the 1930s the government of Japan had to find a way to reduce the costs of raw materials. The ill-fated solution was to attack her neighbors in the Pacific region. During and after World War Two, the inflation rate soared.

From Jim Sinclair's MineSet—Classic Examples of Inflation: After WW2, Japan went through the highest denomination at that time, which was a 75,000,000,000 Yen bank cheque. The Japan wholesale price index (relative to 1 as the average of 1930) shot up to 16.3 in 1943, 127.9 in 1948 and 342.5 in 1951. In the early 1950s, after achieving independence from USA, Japan controlled its own money. Through its rapidly growing export trade, Japan stabilized the Yen quickly.

Now the crucial part that I want to explain is the astrology of Japan at that time. In the 1930s the progressed Venus of Japan's natal astrology chart was direct in motion but slowing down to a (negative cycle) standstill (similar to Zimbabwe in the present day and the US a few decades from now). The complete standstill occurred just about 1947 and her economy was a disaster area and the country in ruins. It is my opinion that as progressed Venus slows down, a nation's money and economy is badly impacted. When the planet Venus in the national horoscope stops moving completely (and this is an astrological measurement, not astronomical) the worst of the crisis hits home.

Lately, Zimbabwe's progressed Venus in her natal horoscope is slowing down in direct motion and will reach a standstill in a few years. The Zim dollar is extinct now and worthless. The nation uses the South Africa Rand and US dollar for trade and business. Everyone has heard of the horror stories to come out of that wretched nation. The government promises to restore the Zim dollar in 2010. Stand back for round two of total chaos if it does.

Weimar Germany natal horoscope had Venus progressed slowing to retrograde (negative cycle) at the time of the hyperinflation. The nation suffered chaotic money problems and the government quickly collapsed later on. A brutal war mongering dictatorship emerged to take advantage of the conditions.

Hold onto your hats. The United States currently direct in motion (positive cycle) Venus in the US natal horoscope is going to slow down. This has never happened before in our history. Now this process takes many decades to complete before a full standstill. But it is not too early to prepare for it. Measures must be taken NOW to avoid a horrible catastrophe which will ruin the lives of every man, woman and child living during the years later this century. The manufacturing base of the USA must be restored. The US must pay off all debts to foreigners. The US must have a balanced trade. Thrift and frugality must be encouraged. The fiat currency system must be eliminated and a sound money standard reintroduced. The Federal government must be downsized. The USA is heading directly into a monster economic storm that puts the 1930s into a league of kindergartners throwing mud pies.

Obviously, if the US goes to war like Japan did to solve these economic problems matters only get worse. That leaves the first solution—the adjusting of living standards and work like we are an emerging market. This method seems distasteful; but it is actually noble to do whatever one can to live an honest life. There is no disgrace to avoid doing harm to others. To save money for the future is good. To learn fine craftsmanship is good and it will be rewarded in time. To devote one's life to honest labor is good.

Politicians do everything in their power to create a heaven on earth—for politicians.

Beware the governmental plutocrat who craves power and control. A cozy relationship exists between government, mass media and banking; more than a little loot has been secured in that regard. The negative Jupiter cycle with its low standard of ethics allows this sort of conspiracy of selfish interests to thrive.

US politicians fear the end of their top of the heap status. It's no secret that debt overwhelms productivity in the States. Almost half the States have serious budget deficits. We import more than we export and we borrow to pay off the difference. Foolish environmental laws forced businesses to shut down and taxes finished off the remainder. Now most former US business is relocated overseas where the political climate is more favorable to the productive class. But this anti business climate here worked for a while because leaders promised to make up the difference as the financial capitol of the world. But it backfired.

It backfired because the unsustainable eventually stumbles. Making money off of other peoples' credit card, auto loan and mortgage debt is really quite uncertain and definitely odd.

Creative accounting produced strange investment vehicles that no one understood. Rating agencies dodged standard accounting rules and approved them for sale to pension funds, etc. No one understood them until they blew up, that is. An alphabet soup of magical potions designed to get something for nothing. We are drowning in a tidal wave of debt and failed leverage. On top of that, the stimulus plans will wipe out the hopes of prosperity of future generations of Americans. The debt load on the future is enormous and growing bigger all the time. There is no way that our present standard of living or life style is sustainable. Our standard of living has been based on borrowing from lenders abroad and unborn generations of Americans for decades. It is unsustainable because the demand for loans increases yearly. The debt service will eventually outweigh everything else. And as I have reported above, the risk of hyperinflation a few decades hence is unavoidable unless drastic monetary changes occur in the meantime.

"Uncle!" cries the economy. Don't just take my word for it, the financial system said so itself, in so many words, by shutting down. The failsafe to an unsustainable system is to come to a complete halt. Indeed, one can rightly say that the financial system behaved according to the program; it came to a screeching halt as soon as the "going bonkers" tripwire was triggered. The economy laughed itself to paralysis the situation was so absurd. The economy was a good sport, up to a point. The economy started laughing and it could not stop, so it went into a coma.

The government is trying to bring it back to life. Turn it back on like a Frankenstein monster kind of thing. Why are their so many zombie movies out of Hollywood lately?

To do whatever it takes to restart the thing. Restart the credit and debt repayment system. Jolt the economy back to "life". But it is simply unsustainable; it will shut down again quickly. Then what? New solutions are needed. The only question is, will the US go to war to preserve the standards of living of our politicians. This is a crucial question. Our politicians are clever. We see it every day. At Christmas eve 2009, discretely, Congress approved an unlimited ceiling of aid for Fannie Mae and Freddie Mac; it may cost taxpayers tens of billions more every year. If a war begins the public attention will be riveted on that and off the financial mess. The politicians will use a war to beat the public into the ground while maintaining a high standard of living for itself.

Does the government really mean it when it says it will do whatever it takes to get the nation on the right track? Probably not.

Nevertheless, someday an administration will mean it and I can say astrologers ought to be included in the program. For the purpose of example I mention two outstanding astrologers in this book. However, there are many more.

Robert Zoller, an astrologer with a history of careful prediction technique and accurate intuition, seems to have nailed down the Islamic Fundamentalist WTC attack of Sept. 11, 2001 His first prediction occurs in the late 1990s. Using his special astrological techniques, he traces the attack to an outside agency; not domestic like Oklahoma City. Curiously he lays the fault to government incompetence even before the attack takes place and he warns of it 3 times ahead of the attack, a year ahead the 3rd time.

In a private letter to me, Robert Zoller's office says the predictions made in the magazine "Nuncius" were under his name but were actually the result of another astrologer's delineation in collaboration with Zoller. This other astrologer remains anonymous to this day and prefers it that way.

Lynne Palmer, noted celebrity astrologer, also predicted (danger of) terrorist attacks on that very day in print in her annual almanac for 2001. She wrote the book in 2000.

Why is there intelligence-gathering failure? From 1994 to 2017 the US natal Mercury is retrograde (negative cycle) in the horoscope of the United States. This is a challenging aspect for any nation with a complex society and high tech security apparatus, rules and regulations. When the planet Mercury is retrograde some degree of accident and confusion prevails; misinformation or no information complicates the ordinary flow of business, transport and communications. So I must agree with the astrologer that American security was flawed on Sept. 11, 2001 and for the few years before while the terrorists were making plans to infiltrate and execute.

This is precisely why an established certified hierarchy of predictive astrologers and psychics must have the ear of national leaders. To leave the affairs of man entirely in the weaker hands of unenlightened elected officials is a recipe for disaster.

Since the planet Mercury in the US natal chart is retrograde now, government plans are most likely flawed or incomplete to deal with fiscal crisis. And worst of all, the ill conceived plans made today may insure the major hyperinflation is a fact of life in the future. This is not a time to leave matters of this importance in the hands of a few politicians and economists who demonstrate incompetence anyway.

Fortunately, correct remedies can be found and applied because the risk of major hyperinflation is a few decades in the future. I would like to see that the disaster is avoided completely to spare the future generations. With right actions taken today, that potential disaster can be minimized. It may already be too late. I don't know. I do know that the US chart works very well in terms of displaying the events in the nation. A runaway spendthrift government that boasts that it will do whatever it takes to control a certain condition that that government itself created is a dangerous government because it thinks that more poison is the cure for the poisoned patient.

As I mentioned before, an instance of minor hyperinflation will occur by 2023. Due to the huge budget deficit and other factors, such as money supply growth, this episode will exceed the inflation scare of the late 1970s, early 80s by several orders of magnitude.

That's what its all about. The nation has to set aside the mediocre academics and narrow-minded scientists. These authority figures are helpless in the face of the new challenges. They are all ill equipped to deal with the rapid pace of change of consciousness. The civilized world is shifting on its psychological axis and this shift is displacing a former mode of thinking. Crazy schemes of getting something for nothing have been accepted as politically correct by the majority; but this thinking is finished. The moral compass is moving.

A Tidal Wave of change is heading our way. Its like the water is being pulled out of the beach and coastline. This is what they call Deflation. The next phase is the reverse. The huge volume of water rushes back to the coast and that will be called the Hyperinflation Event. This will destroy every part of civilization that is unprotected.

Money is like water. Some even call it currency, as in currents of liquidity. As the government stimulus of money adds up, the tidal wave gets more powerful. When the critical mass is reached, all that money will flood back into the market system and Main Street. It will demolish the orderly pricing of goods and services. Just like in Japan, Zimbabwe and in Weimar Germany.

Bailouts have a whole new meaning now.

CHAPTER FOUR

SPIN DOCTORING—MERCURY RETROGRADE NEGATIVE CYCLE

In general, the Mercury cycle concerns itself with accurate and factual information. The positive Mercury cycle promotes reliable information, honest and intelligent discourse. The negative cycle hampers discourse to make it bullying, secretive or misinformed discussion. The truth is concealed and cover stories abound. Statistics are doctored to fit the propaganda. Traces of deceit spawns distrust.

The most recent mercury negative cycle commenced in 1994. Given that it was slowing down a few years earlier this cycle suggests that the policies of the 90s contributed, along with the negative Jupiter cycle, to the demise of the financial system. The government, for example, ordered the banking community to suspend normal fiduciary assessment of mortgage seekers. That is, can the debt be repaid? The result was the subprime disaster we all know about today. Then the government said the subprime problems would not spread past the housing industry. We know how accurate that was.

This and other absurd policies were pushed through despite warnings from more cautious parties.

The collapse of giant Long Term Capital Management two years before the Nasdaq collapse in 2000 should be a conspicuous red flag warning that the formula for derivatives and hedging was loaded with errors. The derivative market has mushroomed while Mercury is retrograde. I consider this an ominous development; all the fail-safes of these dangerous instrument are based on a negative cycle. That means there are probably no safety nets. When that negative cycle is overtaken by the positive cycle in 2017, the derivatives market will fall apart rapidly as the markets implode.

The government also allowed derivative markets to expand recklessly. Attempts to make the derivative markets more transparent and orderly were squashed. The reasons why are buried in the recesses of power politics.

United States border controls were reduced to almost nothing from sheer neglect or the need for neo-slave labor. The government has no solid information about who is in the country beyond citizens and legal immigrants. Agents of the border patrol have been reprimanded or worse for doing their job.

These are just a few prime examples of the inferior decision making at the highest levels that occur when Mercury cycle is negative. Social policy such as this has ruined the economy and created a vast amount of confusion. Simply blaming the bankers or the free market system is unfair and another example how the negative cycle of misleading the public works. The bankers may be guilty of some things but at the end of the day they did not desire to suspend reasonable assurances of being repaid by mortgage holders. Nor did they want their financial products to lose creditworthiness and freeze up the credit markets.

Lets not forget Enron and Worldcom or Bear Stearns, Lehman Brothers, AIG and many more. Federal Reserve Chairman Ben Bernanke said on July 16, 2008, that Fannie Mae and Freddie Mac are "adequately capitalized" and "in no danger of failing." Then-Secretary Treasurer Henry Paulson declared on August 10, 2008, "We have no plans to insert money into either of those two institutions." A number of cabinet members stepped forward to calm the marketplace with reassurances.

Both Fannie and Freddie were nationalized 28 days later, on September 8, 2008. Ben Bernanke claimed on February 28, 2008, "Among the largest banks, the capital ratios remain good and I don't expect any serious problems of that sort among the large, internationally active banks . . ." Henry Paulson added on July 20,

2008, "It's a safe banking system, a sound banking system. Our regulators are on top of it. This is a very manageable situation."

What is wrong with this picture? Were they truly befuddled? Today the Federal government OWNS the banking system. Today the federal public debt is about $40,000 per person.

Lastly, the so-called Patriot Act was created in the Mercury negative time frame. Homeland Security was created at the same time. Most Americans are nervous about these big developments that seem to override ordinary liberties.

Whatever the truth is, it stands to reason that our government needs the assistance of qualified astrologers. But before that, the Federal Reserve Bank and the fiat currency system must be retired. The greatest talents in the world cannot save a house built on quicksand.

There is no substitute for accurate information during times of crisis. Mere economists, in general, don't have the long-term insight necessary to avoid pitfalls, to see the big picture. (The Austrian School of economists impresses me; they do have correct understanding of markets). Intelligence gathering without psychic input is less that accurate or even misleading. Government can't be trusted to steer a ship alone and get it right. It can be done during quiet weather. But control is lost in the storm. I see a nation-wide pool of psychics and astrologers aiding the decision making process of our Constitutional government on every level.

The proper educational curriculum would produce a fine crop of psychics every year. Graduates who have a degree in psychic prediction improve society's chances for survival. Education must change in the future to allow for more talents in the mainstream of society. Imagine if the Executive branch, US Treasury, AIG, Lehman Brothers, Bear Stearns, Citigroup, etc. had psychics on the payroll. None of this mess would have occurred. Imagine a Psychic Security Agency existed. I guarantee 911 would never have happened; psychics would have sounded the alert years ahead of that tragic day. Proof of this exists but it's not a hot mass media topic.

Academia should open its eyes to the real facts about skillful astrologers and psychics. Knee-jerk dismissals in times like these are an insult to all honest scientists and educators. The Establishment must be scrutinized, upgraded, improved and refined.

In 2017 Mercury cycle goes from negative back to positive. When that happens exposure to the light of day of malinvestment commences. Many scandals will erupt. Because of this and other astrological facts, I am afraid that the nation will suffer a serious financial and social calamity. The civil disorder and cessation of the markets will end with mass starvation and hyperinflation in the years to follow. Therefore, I encourage honest politicians, citizens and the press to immediately begin an investigation into the secrets of the Federal Government and the Federal Reserve Bank. Why? If the nasty truths are revealed one by one rather than all at once in 2017, the public may be able to digest it more easily over several years. If the public is assured that honest government will result from these investigations, they will remain patient and supportive. Trust is key here.

Why, even in 2009 an important investigator with the 911 inquiries committee revealed that the report was almost a total lie. More government people should step out of the shadows and tell what they know about the inner workings.

2017 is 7 years away. There is no time to lose.

Watergate was conducted in a civilized manner and the nation went about its business.

Rep. Ron Paul and others push for the audit of the FRB. The entire nation ought to stand with Paul and demand a complete examination of that private bank and every governmental activity and agency, as well. An examination is needed if only because the national debt is increasing exponentially and is it necessary to get to the truth. The retrograde Mercury cycle brings suspicion on every government move.

I hope the mass media applies leverage to the politicians for more honesty and less spin doctoring. The mass media has lost relevance since 1994. That is due to the Internet's more honest information gathering. Indeed, the Internet has surprised a lot of people by opening up new channels of accurate information about history and current events. People blocked out of the mass media can express themselves. The internet is like Tom Paine's "Common Sense".

Gold is called a "barbarous relic". Astrology, like gold, is called the same thing. It is a remnant from a civilization lost in the mists of time. It is one of our non-material connections to the origins of

—

intelligent life on earth. I do not want astrology to be called a science, for that label is too limiting. Gold and astrology are two of the pillars of civilization.

The following two excerpts come from a book by Karen Christino called "The Best of Al H Morrison"—an enlightening book.

The U.S. Horoscope
from a letter of April 11, 1988

It is a superstition to think that all historic events are documented as to the hour and minute of their happening. Astrologically, the birth or founding of nations is that unrecorded hour and minute at which the founders come to consensus, commit themselves to create the new nation.

The birth of the nation came at the Second Continental Congress with the realization that 13 separate nation-states could not collaborate well enough to succeed, and the advice of the Oneida tribe of Native Americans was adopted. The unrecorded hour and minute of that decision was the birth of the nation.

In those times the general population held the view that astrology was both fraud and sin . . . The concealment from the general public of the astrology and astrological practices by some of the founders of U.S.A., the patriots in Philadelphia on July 4, 1776, has been one of the most successful cover-ups in all history . . . The personal correspondence between Franklin and Jefferson has technical astrological symbols written in the margins, by way of making more explicit and adding several layers of meaning/significance to the words they wrote in the body of the letter . . . The official listing of the books now present in the personal library of Thomas Jefferson includes an astrological text, totally useless to anybody other than a practicing astrologer. Benjamin Franklin wrote in his autobiography a clear reference to astrology, in what is obviously a concealment . . . Later, in *Poor Richard's Almanack*, Franklin printed astrological tables, technical material useful to nobody other than astrologers . . . The dates selected in the constitutional convention which framed our present (later-amended) Constitution were all set to favor the national horoscope for the early hours of July 4, 1776 at Philadelphia.

At noon March 4 of any and all years at Philadelphia and at Washington D.C. an anniversary horoscope has the founding national Sun (degree of the zodiac held by Sun in the early hours of the morning of July 4, 1776) on the eastern horizon. Those who are competent in elective astrology recognize this selection of such a ritual as the inauguration of a new president as a primary astrological benefit, available at no other date in any year. Until FDR shifted the inauguration date to a date which forever yields extremely negative astrological aspects to the founding U.S. chart, we had a fair amount of national luck, prestige elsewhere in the world. Example: the Monroe Doctrine was respected.

. . . The cover-up persists; the public does not know that Ronald Reagan was guided by astrology until he finally got into a spot in which he could not personally choose the dates and hours of significant events.

. . . The inauguration date is merely one of many superb examples of very competent traditional elective astrology. The same goes for the establishment of Election Day. The elective astrology there is also explicitly pertinent to the founding horoscope. Only very competent practicing astrologers could have selected that way of dating Election Day.

Inauguration Day
from a letter of January 5, 1992

Franklin Delano Roosevelt installed the Age of Aquarius as our official national astrology. Benjamin Franklin persuaded the Constitutional Convention to have every Inauguration set for noon March 4, stating in rather clear language that his reason was astrological. At noon March 4, the Ascendant will always be about the same zodiac degree as our founding Sun (no matter which wrong chart you favor for the founding of the U.S.A.).

Roosevelt persuaded Congress, the States and the Supreme Court that Inauguration Day should always come on January 20. It is a Constitutional Amendment, 20th such. Thus, we will always inaugurate a new President and his party's apparatus as the Executive Branch of our government with the Sun at 0 (degree of) Aquarius. The Ascendant in all Inauguration charts will always be ±16 Taurus. Translation: money is always to be the top line, all the middle lines, and the bottom line. We have had very choppy luck since that change. We have lost two wars (Korea and Viet Nam) and botched a third (Kuwait/Iraq), become the world's most indebted debtor nation. Our population has changed to include millions of illegal aliens complicating our efforts to cope . . .

End of excerpts.

If I can I will reset inauguration day to March 4 at noon where it belongs.

CHAPTER FIVE

2007-2088 MARS NEGATIVE RETROGRADE CYCLE

The budget deficit grew from 1.2 percent of the economy to 9.8 percent between 2007 and 2009. That's a factor of more than 8 times in two years. Progressed Mars has entered the negative cycle; these bulging deficits are here to stay for a very long time.

I think people will understand why this financial crisis seems to never end if they know a few things. First of all, the United States has been in a gradual decline for decades. The growth and industry planet, progressed Mars, has been slowing down for many years (while still in positive cycle) and began the negative (retrograde) cycle in 2007.

When Mars began to slow the US oil production peaked. The growth rate by population also peaked. Politics entered the work area; for example, a federal government agency was created to help disgruntled employees file law suits against employers, affirmative action, more "red-tape" on business owners, anti-smoking, anti-discrimination rules, work-place safety, bi-lingual requirements, environmental issues and more. These social engineering concepts produced nothing and in many cases reduced output or real productivity. At least one study in the 1980s claimed that employees who smoke on the job were more productive than those who did not smoke.

Eventually, oil import expenses ruined the US trade balance. With dollars going to foreigners for oil, there was less for domestic improvements. So, naturally, the Federal Reserve, Treasury Dept. and Congress printed more paper money to compensate. The debt ceiling always went higher. To keep the budget deficit within bounds Congress increased taxes. Business fled the US for better treatment elsewhere and stateside companies reined in salaries or employment. Prices went higher. People depended on more government assistance to make ends meet. And so on and so forth in a vicious cycle of desperation.

The Mars (drive, industry) negative cycle coincides with demographic predictions for the US. The worker (young) age groups are shrinking against the aging retired population. A strong surge in retirements will occur over the next 25 to 30 years while the birth rate is flat. Demographic analysts agree that a nation's prosperity rests upon the young energetic workers' shoulders. Or an aging worker must work longer and delay retirement. Taxes to pay for the support of the elderly come from the payrolls of the employed. The relentless march towards "golden years" retirement is built into our social and cultural fabric. Fewer and fewer workers support more and more retirees. This is not sustainable.

Mars entering negative cycle directly or indirectly produced other conditions like the increase in sexual confusion, bitter gender alienation and resentments, mental disorders, illiteracy, boredom, the craving for cheap excitement, the search for "fun" jobs, the constant drug and alcohol abuse, the loss of manufacturing jobs, the growth of the prisoner population, the decay of infrastructure, disrespect for private property, graffiti, unprotected national borders, the lack of willingness to win wars, the rise in gambling and lotteries and the hot pursuit of freebies from the government, etc. The negative cycle lasts until 2088.

The decline is very real and indicated in the astrology of the United States horoscope as stationary to retrograde (negative) Mars. Here is the prognosis. The US will be a second rate nation for at least 100 years as Mars continues to retrograde in the US horoscope. There is no possible way out of this fact of national life. Will the government demand by law that citizens have more babies? Will the government demand that citizens and other people stop asking for freebies and assistance? Not likely. But something positive must be done to modify and reverse the deterioration of standard of living.

According to *Fortune* magazine, 40 percent of American employees in the 21st century will be "contingency" workers. This means that they will never work permanently for any company. They will continue to move from job to job, earning less money than full-time employees and accruing few, if any, benefits. The employee will be doing a completely different job requiring completely different skills on a regular basis.

I think that that percentage will be higher.

If things get really bad the elderly may be shipped off to remote corners of the globe where costs of living are a tiny fraction of what they are here. This is not an appealing thought.

Mars represents drive and industry; these things are not apparent in the US today. This is why I recommend that the government shrink itself voluntarily. The cost to support a big central government such as exists today will destroy the exhausted taxpayers. And the tax savings must be directed to restart US industry, farming and modest sized factory production of essential goods. Renewable energy infrastructure also needs building.

Unfortunately, the trend appears to slam against my advice. Total government employment has increased substantially while private sector jobs are lost. Indeed, government workers make about 45 percent more in salary and benefits than private sector workers. If this trend continues, the United States will collapse into a third world state of poverty and all employment will end. Why? Because the government cannot print enough money to pay for everyone on its payrolls without bankrupting the nation. Yet this is what the government seems to want to do.

I think hapless politicians "hope" that "relief" is just around the corner. They think that they avoided a big recession or economic collapse in 2008-09. They think that the stimulus bailouts did the trick. They also think that the housing market will recover, mortgage lenders will find work and home builders will build. Perhaps they think the government can provide employment for all the rest. Just borrow more and tax more. The government provides the food, clothing and shelter and entertainment as well as a job for life. They must ask themselves late at night, "Why can't the private sector provide job security just like the government can?"

The US is now an emerging nation with a fading vision of a once dominant world power. That's what the planetary cycles are saying. Washington DC still plays a hand it was dealt 50 years ago. I use the word "emerging" for lack of a better one. A nation that has no growth or output in the normal way must recreate itself. It must return to basics. I think agriculture, renewable energy and high tech electronics are the way to go for our emerging economy. Maintenance and repair of infrastructure and communications networks needed as well. Anyone at any age can participate in farming. Can we export food, basic goods and ingenious high-tech inventions cheaply? Can we make it a business friendly nation once more?

The question about exports includes the cooperation of importing nations. Will the international bankers coerce foreign governments to ignore our products in retaliation for the termination of the Federal Reserve Bank? History shows that these banker elites are capable of most anything to get their way. Consider Pres. Andrew Jackson's struggle to rid the US of the international banker clique's central bank.

Taxation should be reduced and laws restrictive to business should be removed from the books. For example, the minimum wage laws and the laws against employing children are unnecessary now. They are unnecessary because we are becoming a different country.

We don't need universal education churning out lawyers or investment bankers and other useless occupations. In fact, we don't need a public school system. It's just a waste of billions to produce millions of illiterates. Young people don't want to learn pointless information; they want to get out there and earn money. They have a basic feel for what's going on. Drop the minimum wage laws and a million jobs will open up overnight. Within a year millions more will find work as the economy reawakens.

It is appalling that children are drugged so that they don't disrupt the classroom. The reality is that they are bored and want to leave. It is better to channel that youthful energy into productive uses.

We are not going to try to impress the rest of the world with our progressive liberal culture any more. Survival is at stake. The nation must work harder just to pay the interest on the debt outstanding.

And we must pay our debts or forever feel shame. We have to be resourceful, creative and waste nothing. We have to drop unnecessary fears about using nuclear energy, natural gas and coal. We have to decide how to reduce the Federal government and cut costs.

The US is not going to be a major player on the international stage any longer. This will be more and more apparent with the passage of time. The faster that this fact is acknowledged politically, the better for the nation as a whole. Our generosity and foreign aid ought to be reduced or eliminated entirely. Membership with international organizations should cease. We won't have the wherewithal to help others for a very long time. Most foreign aid goes into the pockets of crooked leaders. How many billions do the crooked politicians in the Middle East and Africa have stashed away in Swiss banks? The starving national gets crumbs.

Better we accept that "charity begins at home" and help our own citizens get through these long decades of struggle and limitations with dignity and proper nutrition, housing and other basic needs taken care of. I am not recommending a welfare state. I am suggesting that taxes must be small and let people take care of themselves and each other on a personal or local level. Let the rest of the world fend for itself now. We should also consider removal from the United Nations, as this organization is just a money pit. The whole notion of taxation for foreign aid is highly questionable.

Taxation to bail out the international bankers and inept businesses is outrageous wastefulness.

If the government in Washington pretends that it's business as usual and high taxation will take care of every problem, then it is possible that our nation will sink into a third world state. This would be a true disaster because it almost insures that a Civil War will break out. 2017 is a crucial year regarding civil order and calm. It is imperative that the Federal government goes on a major diet of size, duty and personnel. The consequences of more massive debt is a poor third world type of country with constant bickering and squabbling over scarce goods.

The negative Mars cycle has influenced the destruction of many productive sectors that sustained the nation in years gone by. This is why the tax base is affected. This is why new times call for new industries. But the federal government cannot suck all the money out of the economy. The negative Jupiter cycle seems to encourage that; it's easier to tax than to understand widespread dynamics of change. Government produces nothing of value unless you like to read velocity statistics while you plummet into the crevice. (That statistic will be seasonally adjusted.) Wealth for new business startups must circulate in the economy to fertilize the natural free enterprise system.

The State of Oklahoma is already pursuing a lawful Tenth Amendment-style reduction of Washington's intrusion into its State functions. All US States should follow the example of Oklahoma. Realistically, the States must do more, as best they can. Let the Federal only provide for the things as the Constitution clearly denotes and nothing more. This is a sign of the weakened negative Jupiter influence—a refusal to support the goals of big government advocates.

Rep. Paul Ryan, Rep. Wisconsin, has a solid bill that would reduce government and maintain the flow of wealth in the economy. His Roadmap is viewable online.

I reject secession as a remedy. But little can be done to stop it as long as the Federal Reserve and international banking continues to call the shots. To burden generations of yet unborn Americans with 70 or more trillion dollars worth of debt is scandalous. Is this insuring domestic tranquility? (One trillion dollars deficit times 70 years equals 70 trillion.)

How to put real meaning back into living? Humans must have a challenge, it seems to be built into the genetic code. A massive network of small farms could be designed and built to serve the towns and cities. Transport of food must be realistic and continuous in a nation of limited resources. Essential services must have back-up systems. Our challenge is obvious—get back to basics and self-reliance.

These are examples of worthwhile endeavors that can keep Americans employed for a very long time. Solar and hydropower installations are other engineering projects to consider. All these modes of collecting renewable and non-renewable energy work as a team, like alternating inputs, filling in the gaps of one another. In some parts of the country geo-thermal energy is abundant.

The fantastic consumer economy of years past gradually fades away; and imports shrink. New industries and old manufacturing of ordinary goods rebuilds itself naturally in the free enterprise marketplace. Trading may be the order of the day for a long while. America is an emerging economy and money has a different look.

From a risk management standpoint we have to put our engineers and scientists to work on these basic problems. The future will be very bleak if there is no indoor plumbing, heat, hot water or light. The greatest danger is the US sinking into despondency. The next great danger is public resistance to farm work. How awful that the US loses its cheap fossil fuel just at the time that it loses its industrial base. But we have to find the strength within to go on. Think of this as reliving the pioneer days. Life was harsh but it was not impossible to survive and thrive.

Diabetes cases decrease when junk food is no longer produced. Universal healthcare will morph into self-care. I would read up on herbal remedies and alternative medicines. Medical people who understand the tried and true Eastern methods of healing are important. Its time we cease treating the symptoms and target cure at the source of the problems. Yes, this means the end of the big pharma industry; but so what. From the looks of things today, drugs generally didn't produce any better living or health. Added to that are persistent rumors of a suppressed cure for cancer. No, big pharma is not the answer to a healthier life.

I would hope that the auto makers can convert to electric vehicles in short order. And the infrastructure of charging stations must be built. But it seems unlikely. Motorization declines. It may be likely that fewer people will drive. Conservation means that stores will close early; more time spent at home. Television will have more "how to do it" programming. The most rewarded will be those who know how to repair appliances, plumbing and lamps, etc. New models of appliances will not appear so quickly anymore. The era of fast remodeling is over. Making do and reusing is a must. The era of explosive innovation peaked in the 1980s and 90s when transiting Pluto was in the sign of Scorpio. Pluto rules innovation or renewal and it transits Scorpio the fastest of all 12 signs. Pluto left Scorpio in 1996. There will be some innovation, just not the rapid-fire kind we have come to expect. So, the repairman will be highly paid. Pluto returns to Scorpio around 2230.

Welfare is not the answer to this problem. It works for a while (as we have witnessed over the past few decades) but eventually hyperinflation crushes the world. Welfare can't be sustained because at some point the money taken from the wealthy runs out. Then the middle class drops into the welfare rolls. Then fake money is printed to cover shortfalls. This in turn causes prices to rise faster and faster and the economy spins out of control. Then the politicians find scapegoats at random and labels it "greedy".

The US has used welfare to keep the society humming along. However, the psychology behind that method is decaying. The government will not be welfare oriented in the future. By 2035, when progressed US Sun enters Aries from Pisces (traditional sign of self-sacrificial altruism), the routine sob-story psychology will change to self-sufficiency or self-reliance for all. There will be no government handouts. Government will be much smaller, too. (Government is the largest welfare recipient.)

Just for this reason alone it is essential that tens of millions of small businesses, factories and farms sprout up nationwide to absorb the workers dropped from the welfare rolls. The economic changes Americans face in the coming years will dwarf the credit-housing-debt crisis of today.

The only solution for America is to start over as if it was 1790 again. Not doing so might direct us to 1861 instead.

What about tourism? Good sources of foreign exchange are tourist visitors' spending money. Our new nation will be a curiosity for the rest of the world. An emerging nation with full employment is an inspiration to others. Our landmarks ought to be preserved for the sake of tourist attractions. Some Americans may take pride in keeping Las Vegas functioning, for example, even if we don't have time for that entertainment ourselves. Fifth Avenue, Rodeo Drive, etc. should be preserved.

CHAPTER SIX

URANUS AT 8 DEGREES OF GEMINI

I want to emphasize a fact of the US horoscope in terms of the recurrences of Uranus by transit to a specific degree of the sign of Gemini. Gemini 7 degrees 32 minutes is the Ascendant of the standard US natal chart. It also happens that Uranus is conjunct this ascendant at 8 degrees 53 minutes of the sign. The following key events occurred when Uranus was at 8 degrees of Gemini by transit (tropical zodiac). The planet Uranus has a period or orbit in time of about 84 years.

The Jamestown colony was founded in 1607 near what is now Chesapeake Bay. In 1608 Uranus by transit was at 8 degrees of Gemini. Some British investors wanted a base from which to seek gold and suitable territory for future settlements. Things went bad almost immediately. Disputes over who was in charge were common. Battles with the local natives were frequent and deadly. Many settlers died of bad drinking water and poor sanitation. A scandal involving one leader accused of atheism was hushed so as not to frighten away future English investors. Jamestown settlers blamed him for the mass deaths by bringing down the wrath of God. One of their hand picked leaders was Capt. John Smith. He was a captive of the local Indian tribe during this fiasco. Chief Powhattan initiated him into the tribe. Smith secured supplies from the natives. But he lied to Powhattan about the purpose of the settlement. The colony survived when more settlers arrived with provisions. Friendly relations with the natives decayed when Smith returned to England.

Aside, Montreal was founded by Jacques Cartier that same year.

Salem, Massachusetts 1692, Uranus at 8 degrees of Gemini.

Feb 28, The Salem witch hunts began.

Jun 10, Bridget Bishop was hanged in Salem, Mass., for witchcraft. This was the first official execution of the Salem witch trials.

Aug 19, Five women were hanged in Salem, Massachusetts after being convicted of the crime of witchcraft. Fourteen more people were executed that year and 150 others are imprisoned.

Sep 19, Giles Corey was pressed to death for standing mute and refusing to answer charges of witchcraft brought against him. He is the only person in America to have suffered this punishment.

In 2006 the governor of Massachusetts signed legislation exonerating 5 women executed in the Salem witch trials of 1692, whose names had not yet been cleared.

Fear, hysteria and death are the characteristics of this amazing and intense fury. The feelings and passions that were exposed resonate to this day. The accusers, all women and girls, become virtual celebrities and break themselves out of the pattern of ordinary life of repressed females in Puritan America.

8th degree of Gemini is occupied by Uranus in the Declaration of Independence signing of July 4, 1776. This is also the Ascendant of the nations birth chart. Almost no one believed a revolution could succeed until it actually happened. Most regarded it as an audacious and foolish campaign.

Now get a load of this: 8th degree of Gemini is occupied by Uranus in the Declaration of Independence of the Confederate States of America signing on February 8, 1861. What is the power of the 8th degree Uranus in Gemini? Fear, hysteria, bloodshed and cruelty reach epic proportions.

In 1944 Uranus again occupied 8 of Gemini. The communists and the fascists went at each other on American soil. The Great Depression lifted. The war overseas was a great opportunity for the government to distract Americans from their economic woes and gain full employment. Roosevelt stopped supplying Japan with oil in 1941 July (McCollum's Action H). The only other source of oil for Japan was in Indonesia/Borneo, south of Hawaii and Pearl Harbor, US naval base. Put two and two together.

Was Roosevelt a genius in this respect? Did he follow the movement of planets? Did he expect Revolution in America? He scooped up and detained the US Japanese citizens quickly. But was he more worried about something else?

When fascism comes to America, it will be wrapped in the flag, carrying a cross.—Sinclair Lewis, author of *It Can't Happen Here*, 1935

In 1927, Evangeline Adams, famous US astrologer, predicted a world war involving the US in 1942,43 and 44. She specifically utilized the Uranus cycle in the US chart. She said the war would start because of religious, racial and political reasons. Roosevelt must have heard about this because she was widely quoted in her day. In that same lecture she correctly predicted the stock market crash of 1929.

Here are some interesting bits of history during the Uranus transit around 8 degrees of Gemini.

1944, Jan 19 In England Helen Duncan (1896-1956), a Scottish spiritualist in Portsmouth, was arrested for informing an audience of the sinking of two British warships long before the news was officially made public. She was found guilty of witchcraft and jailed for nine months. When re-elected in 1951, Churchill repealed the 1735 witchcraft act but Duncan's conviction was never quashed. In 2007 her granddaughter launched a fresh campaign to gain a posthumous pardon for Britain's last convicted witch.

Jun 6, Cherokee tribal members communicated via radios in their native language on the Normandy beaches.

Jun 20, The US Congress chartered the Central Intelligence Agency (CIA).

Jul 1, Delegates from 44 countries began meeting at Bretton Woods, N.H., where they agreed to establish the International Monetary Fund and the World Bank. The US hosted an international conference at Bretton Woods, N.H., to deal with international monetary and financial problems. The talks resulted in the creation of the International Monetary Fund (IMF) and the World Bank in 1945.

The Bretton Woods institutions also include the United Nations and the General Agreement on Tariffs and Trade, later renamed the World Trade Organization (WTO). The agreement was a gold exchange standard and only the US was required to convert its currency into gold at a fixed rate, and only foreign central banks were allowed the privilege of redemption. (In 1983 Michael Moffitt authored "The World's Money: Int'l. Banking from Bretton Woods to the Brink of Insolvency." In 1997 Catherine Caufield wrote "Masters of Illusion: The World Bank and the Poverty of Nations.")

1945, February 18, U.S. Marines stormed ashore at Iwo Jima. Navajo code talkers used their native language to communicate by radio on Japanese troop movements.

The next time Uranus occupies 8th degree of Gemini is the year 2027-28. This happens to be the same year that the negative Jupiter cycle comes to an end. If the international bankers and their allies in Congress opt to fight it out with the forces of sound dollar reform and free markets I expect a civil war in the US. But it will be a guerilla war in every city and town, not a State vs State civil war. It may be the Dept. of Homeland Security against the people. Or, the US government may decide to wage war against various enemies around the world in the hope that Americans will once again be distracted from the chicanery of the banker class and their central banking strongholds.

On a very serious note, Washington, DC could be destroyed by a nuclear bomb in 2028. This is the signal from the 2028 Vernal Equinox chart for the capitol. I would be very afraid to start a war that has this extremely dire prognosis.

Looking at 2027 minor US progressions, an ugly pattern develops that is reminiscent of 1861. I refer to minor Uranus isolated from the rest of the planets and in bad aspect to Pluto. This is a signal that some States want to break with the rest of the Union. Added to the confusion there may be a serious sickness infecting the population. Minor progressed Neptune is also isolated and progressed Mars afflicts it. Mars afflicting Neptune occurred in 1917-18 as a fatal influenza gripped the country. Neptune was also in bad aspect to the Moon's nodes in 1918; Neptune is thus again in 1927. The United States suffers great stresses for these years. This is on top of the potential for serious inflation in the early years of the decade.

There is another possibility with regard to Neptune. And that is self-induced hibernation with chemicals. If this sort of product is created, people with enough money to pay for it could be interred in bombproof secure vaults underground for X number of years. I assume they would take their gold with them. This is a high tech infrastructure with sensors taking readings of the outside world, both atmospheric and digital news via satellite. The computer brain behind this will know when to release the wake up call signal.

If the Federal Reserve Bank is defunct, free markets are restored, and the US has a sound money currency and if astrologers have the ears of the leadership in that time, I am confident that the US will avoid calamity. It seems most important that the leadership has the confidence of the public. Trust in the government needs to be restored between now and then. Sage counsel of astrologers and psychics is the glue that will hold our nation together.

The reader now understands what we are up against. The choice is yours.

CHAPTER SEVEN

UNITED STATES AND FOREIGN SOLAR ECLIPSES

Eclipses generally indicate where on earth dangers exist. Eclipses can foretell earthquakes, tsunamis, political upheavals, terrorist attacks, wars and so on. I have studied eclipses and eclipse paths for years. A lot of information can be gleaned from eclipse paths and if correctly analyzed, many lives can be saved with proper safe guards in place.

I am concerned about two immediate total solar eclipses over the United States. The first one is in May of 2012, the second occurs in August, 2017.

The May 2012 eclipse (image 1) starts in southern China and affects the east coast of China, Japan, Korea, Alaska, the US West Coast, San Francisco in particular, and travels southeast to West Texas where the path ends. What makes this eclipse so compelling is that it actually travels over most the "ring of fire" volcanic zone of the northern Pacific Ocean. And it then moves inland north of San Francisco. Furthermore, it affects those nations that are most willing to purchase US debt, like Treasury bonds. They fund our way of life.

Tensions increase around the Southwestern states border areas. (Earthquakes and social unrest increased in Sichuan and Xinjiang provinces, China during solar eclipses in 2008 and 2009).

Experts insist that San Francisco is due for another earthquake within 40 or so years. The Hayward Fault line in particular is ripe for adjustment. I predict an earthquake near San Francisco in 2012. Because the eclipse passes over the Pacific Ocean fault zones, I predict seismic activity, earthquakes and tsunamis near and around the north Pacific, Alaska and the West Coast. All measures to protect the public need to be readied and brought up to date.

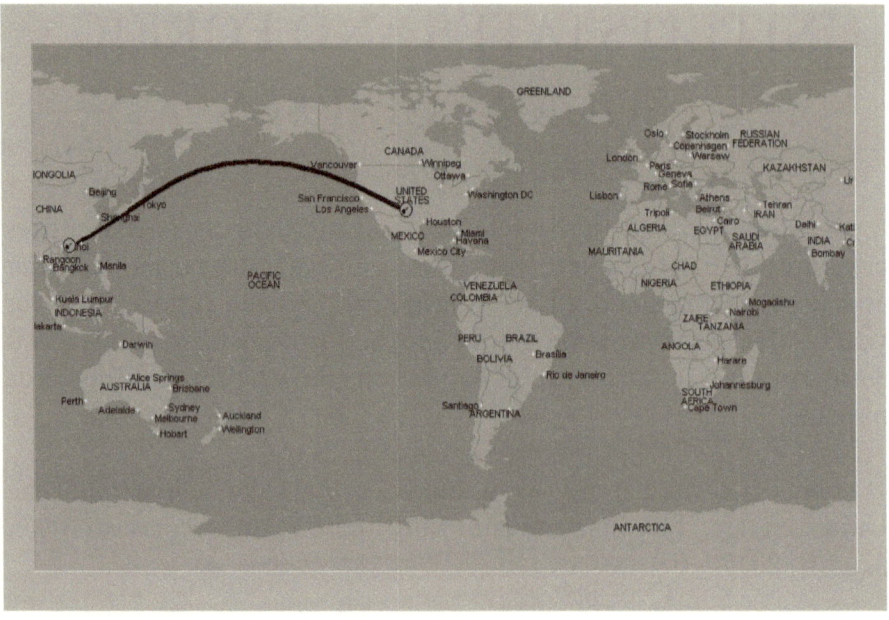

The other eclipse path (image 2) is near Washington DC. It travels South Eastward from Oregon to South Carolina in August 2017. The last eclipse to cross the entire US was in June 1918. That year the nation was afflicted by the Spanish Flu epidemic that killed hundreds of thousands of people. Certain aspects might indicate that a major epidemic will erupt in 2017. The City of Los Angeles may burn or be destroyed in an eruption and fire. Could it be yet another earthquake? The fault lines are certainly vulnerable during this year as they were in 2012. Another possibility is Civil War in the years afterward. In 1865 at the end of the Civil War a total solar eclipse path traversed the nation. There will be stresses in the nation from time to time due to changing conditions of economics, labor and agriculture. Political dissidents and extreme factions will push and argue for advantages or power.

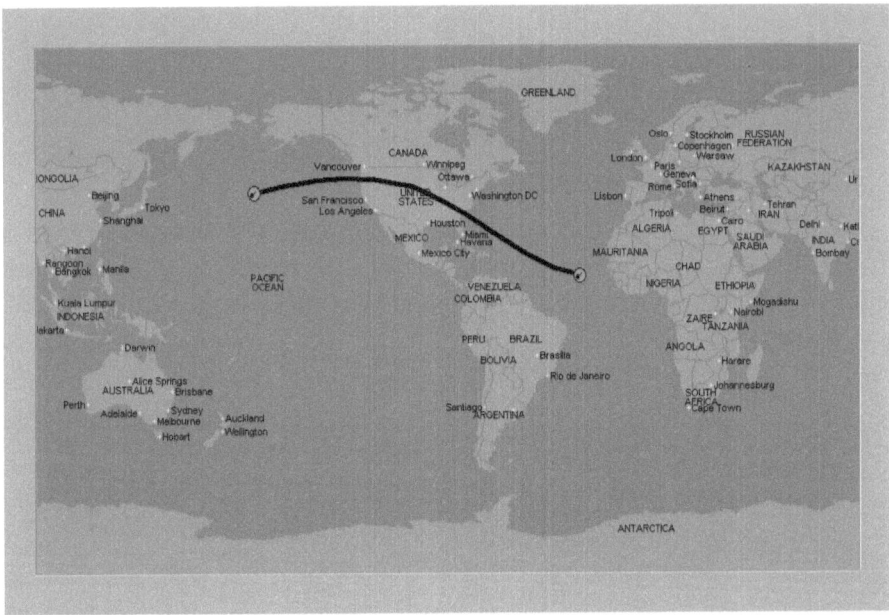

I want to mention an eclipse that occurred in 1999. Image 3 solar eclipse path ties together so much of current world history. It occurred August 11, 1999. This eclipse was partially visible on the east coast of the US although the path of totality is off the coast. It says to me that September 11 attack could have been prevented.

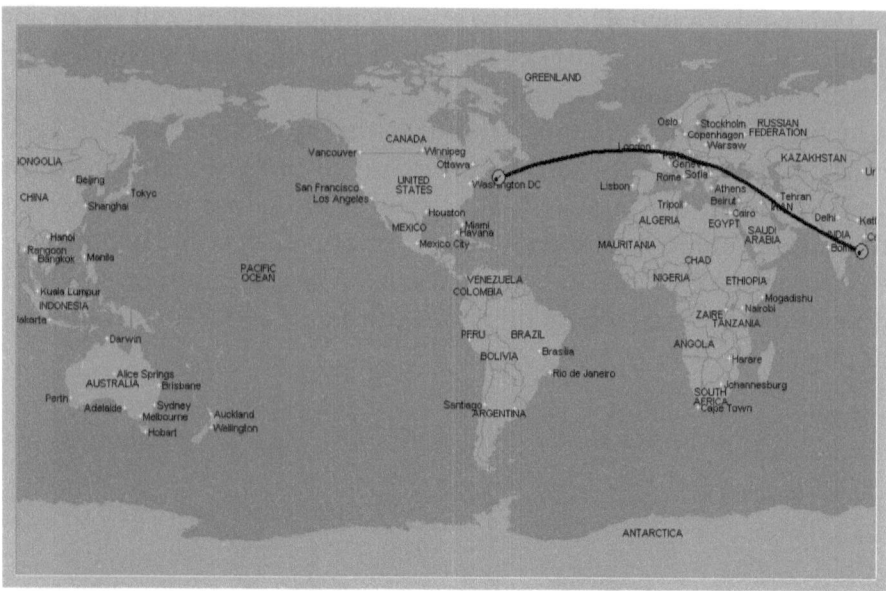

Looking much further ahead we have this solar eclipse on April 8, 2024. Image 4 invites a number of questions. Will Americans overrun Mexico in the search for food? Will there be a war? Who will the leadership be?

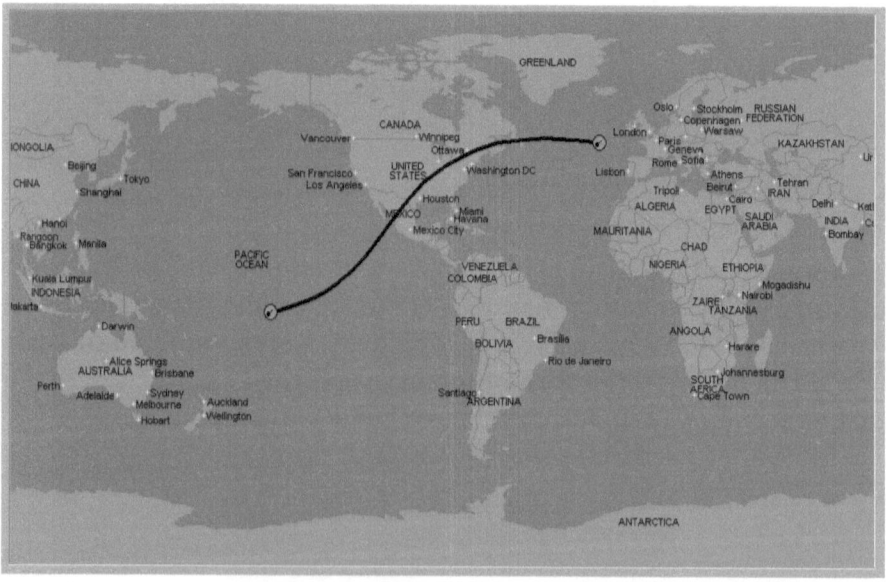

Now I want to present these as a composite on the map in image 5.

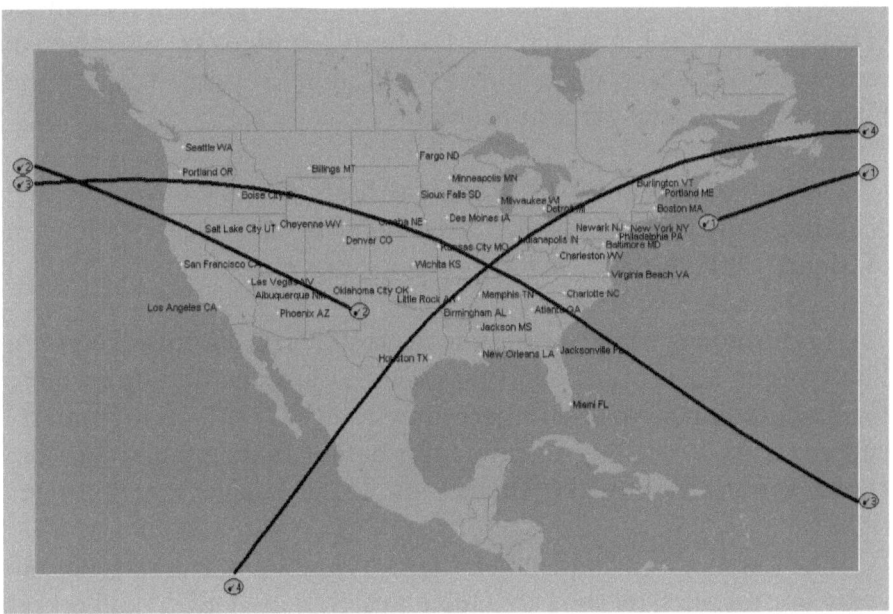

All these solar eclipses occur within a 25 year span of time. Intense. The aggregation says to me that the US is being attacked from several different approaches and stratagems. Everything we do now must be done with strict regard for preservation of liberty and capital. The US is vulnerable to all sorts of treachery from international bankers and financiers and their allies. The wealth of the US is being transferred to foreign parties under the veil of globalism and/or shoring up the markets. The story line is always very plausible and appeals to emotions; but it is fake. It is very likely the credit crisis is pre-arranged (or pushed off a cliff intentionally)—a huge lie and setup for emergency funds in astronomical amounts (to disappear). The sooner the FRB is audited the better.

Interestingly, the US might be a conduit to steal the wealth of Asia, China and Japan as well. They invest their trade surplus with us. The trap is the US Treasury Paper sold at bond auctions. We are talking about trillions of dollars.

Against their will, the taxpayers are responsible for the losses in the faux capitalist system. This is terrorizing. I would invoke the anti-terrorism laws. On Feb. 17, 1950 James Paul Warburg told the US Senate that the nation would be absorbed by a global government of bankers such as himself. A colossal heist is underway. The place to start would be a thorough audit of the Federal Reserve Bank of the US and each central bank in Europe.

Getting back to the West Coast I will discuss an earthquake that occurred at the Hayward fault. That report from the Insurance Journal of March, 2008 follows.

An earthquake of 6.8 magnitude or greater on California's Hayward Fault, in the heart of the San Francisco Bay area, could impact more than 5 million people and impact more than $1.5 trillion in property and contents, according to new information from members of the 1868 Hayward Earthquake Alliance and Risk Management Solutions (RMS).

The last major earthquake on the Hayward Fault was in 1868, 140 years ago: research by the U.S. Geological Survey (USGS) and others indicate the past five such earthquakes have been 140 years apart on average. So an earthquake on this fault is increasingly likely.

If the 1868 earthquake were to reoccur today, RMS estimates total economic losses to residential and commercial properties would likely exceed $165 billion. Other factors, such as fire, damage to infrastructure and related disruption would substantially increase the loss.

In marked contrast to Hurricane Katrina where uninsured losses were approximately 60 to 70 percent of total economic losses, more than 95 percent of projected Hayward Fault earthquake residential losses and 85 percent of commercial losses would be uninsured, the Alliance and RMS indicated.

"Bay Area residents, businesses and local governments need to take action now to reduce future losses. The public understands this and has repeatedly supported bond measures for well-planned seismic upgrade projects, such as the ongoing retrofit of BART and the Hetch Hetchy system," said Mary Lou Zoback, earthquake expert from RMS.

"Public and private organizations have already invested over $30 billion to retrofit or replace vulnerable buildings and infrastructure, but more needs to be done," said Tom Brocher, seismologist with the USGS. Until the Bay Bridge and BART undergo major retrofits, they remain vulnerable to earthquakes and more than 180,000 daily commuters who currently use them could face having to take overtaxed alternate routes for months.

Similarly, until the Hetch Hetchy aqueduct system upgrade is complete, earthquake-related activity could cut off water for 2.4 million Bay Area residents, according to a recent report by the Bay Area Economic Forum.

"People should realize there is a possibility that they won't be able to drive home from work or pick up their children from school," said Jeanne Perkins from the Association of Bay Area Governments. "A Hayward Fault earthquake could close 1,100 roads, including 900 in Alameda County alone."

Oakland and San Francisco international airports and nearly all the region's port facilities are built on materials prone to earthquake damage. As a result, the capacity to deliver the goods needed to support recovery would be significantly diminished. "We hope that this information will promote greater awareness among the general population and will encourage businesses and lifeline operators to achieve greater resiliency in our infrastructure," said Keith Knudsen, a representative of the Earthquake Engineering Research Institute (EERI).

While the projected consequences of a Hayward Fault earthquake are staggering, and similar to that of the 1868 earthquake, authors of this research are encouraged by the interest that residents and community leaders are showing in mitigation and preparedness. "We hope that our research will facilitate more informed decision making on the part of local officials," said Brocher.

The research authors include Thomas Brocher, U.S. Geological Survey, Keith Knudsen, URS Cooperation, Mary Lou Zoback, Risk Management Solutions, Jeanne Perkins, Association of Bay Area Governments, Margaret Hellweg, University of California, Berkeley, William Savage, U.S. Geological Survey, Kathy Bailey, California Governor's Office of Emergency Services.

The authors are also members of the 1868 Hayward Earthquake Alliance *http://www.1868alliance.org*.

For interest's sake, here is the eclipse that occurred around the time of the last Hayward Fault earthquake on October 21, 1868. That solar eclipse occurred on Oct. 19, 1865.

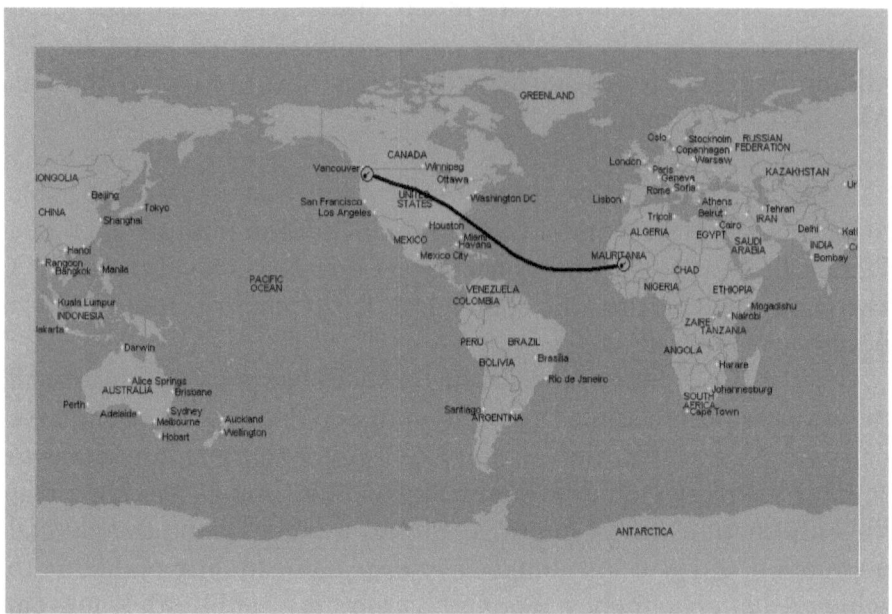

Finally, what happens to a tight geographical area that is subject to a number of solar eclipses within a short span of time? Lets take a close look at a composite of three solar eclipses that traversed over South East Asia (Viet-Nam, Cambodia and Laos) in the 1950s. These solar eclipse paths occurred within 3 years. Take a look at Image 7.

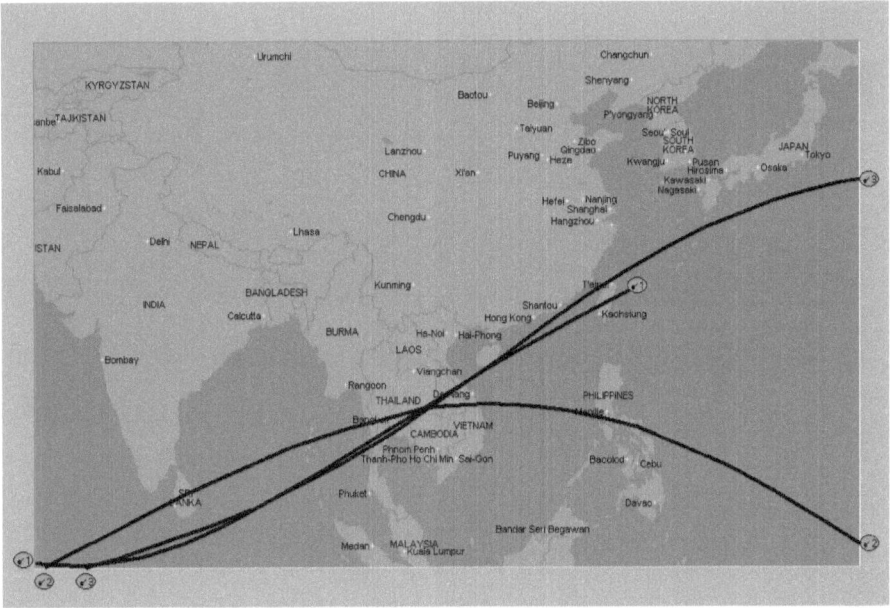

—END—

www.ingramcontent.com/pod-product-compliance
Lightning Source LLC
Chambersburg PA
CBHW030010190526
45157CB00014B/1903